Pat,
Enjoy and I could not have asked for a better sister.
love,
Marian

SEVEN OAKS

Seven Oaks Golf Course and Colgate University campus. Courtesy of the Marian Blain Collection.

SEVEN OAKS

A History of Golf at Colgate University

JIM FORD

UPSTATE INSTITUTE AT COLGATE UNIVERSITY

HAMILTON, NEW YORK 13346

JIM FORD is a native of Madison, NY, and attended Madison Central School and Oneonta State, with his Master's work done at Colgate University. After 34 years teaching junior high history, he has embarked on a new career publishing local history books which have included a history of the Town of Madison; *Sweet Cider Days: A History of Mott's in Bouckville, New York*; *The Pride of Cidertown: A History of the Bouckville Summits Baseball Team, 1866–1935*; plus a number of history articles. He now writes about the golf course he loves.

Copyright © 2013 by Jim Ford, Hamilton, NY 13346
All Rights Reserved

ISBN-10: 0912568259
ISBN-13: 978-0-912568-25-6

Library of Congress Cataloging-in-Publication Data
Ford, Jim.
Seven Oaks : a history of golf at Colgate University / Jim Ford.
pages cm
ISBN 978-0-912568-25-6 (alk. paper)
1. Colgate University–Golf–History. I. Title.
GV969.5.C65F67 2013
796.35209747'64–dc23
2013006873

The paper used in this publication meets the minimum requirements of American National Standard for Information Sciences—Permanence of Paper for Printed Library Materials, ANSI/NISO Z39.48-1992 ∞™

Printed in the United States of America

I am proud to dedicate this history of golf at Colgate University to two individuals who have had a great influence on golf in our community and have also had a positive effect on my personal life as well

The first is Marian (Burke) Blain. Marian has served as golf professional at Seven Oaks for the past thirty-one years. She is a native of Hamilton and a member of a family that did so much to help obtain the beautiful course which we now enjoy.

I remember Marian as a young girl when I worked in the original pro shop at Seven Oaks. She always had the big smile and was ready to challenge any of the boys to a match. That competitive spirit allowed her to become the first female to play on a boy's varsity team at Hamilton and continued with her throughout her college play and mini-tour events.

Marian never forgets the name of a member, alumnus, or even an infrequent visitor to the course. She continually strives to promote golf in Hamilton and also in our Central New York region.

Secondly, I would be remiss if I did not also include Thomas Parnell in this dedication. Following my graduation from nearby Madison Central School, Tom was good enough to offer me a job at the course. We worked side-by-side in the old Pro Shop at a time when the new back nine was opening for play. Working with me was not an easy task for Tom because I had never been to a golf course and had to learn everything on a day-to-day basis. But he was patient with me and I have always cherished the experience.

Tom was not only a mentor but a friend. The lessons that he taught me carried over to my own teaching career. Tom realized that we had a unique championship course and worked diligently to carry on the efforts of William Reid, Everett Barnes, and his professional predecessor, James Dalgety.

Contents

        Acknowledgments   IX

        Introduction   XI

ONE   The Colgate Family and Seven Oaks   1

TWO   Golf Begins in Hamilton   2

THREE   Gene Sarazen, Robert Trent Jones, and a Golf Course Controversy   18

FOUR   The 1940s and Seven Oaks During World War II   31

FIVE   The 1950s—Plans for a Course Are Pushed Forward   40

SIX   The 1960s and Construction of the Back Nine   57

SEVEN   The 1970s and 1980s—Tournaments Highlight Events at the Course   72

EIGHT   The 1990s to the Present   82

Acknowledgments

Without the help of the following individuals the story of Seven Oaks could not have been told. Their willingness to share information has been greatly appreciated.

Darwin "Stub" Baker Performed construction work for the driving range, erosion control of stream banks, and construction of the forward tees

Marian Blain Seven Oaks Golf Professional, 1982 to present

Jack Blanchard Colgate '60

Pat Burke Former member of Seven Oaks

Patty Caprio Director of Leadership Giving at Colgate

Dick Carroll Member of Seven Oaks and former assistant golf coach at Hamilton Central School

Susan Cerasano Professor of English at Colgate and Director of the Colgate University Press

Cindy Chamberlain Administrative Assistant to the Athletic Director at Colgate

Bob Cornell Colgate Sports Information Director, retired

Charlie Dawkins Member of Seven Oaks

Will Delano Colgate 2013, member of the Colgate Golf Team

Bob Deming Colgate '57, 1977 N.C.A.A. Tournament Co-Chairman, former Athletic Director at Colgate, retired

Lisa Diehl Administrative Assistant, Athletic Communications

Julie Dudrick Project Director, Upstate Institute at Colgate

Fred Dunlap Colgate '50, Director of Athletics and football coach at Colgate, retired

Dick Eades Former member of Seven Oaks

Jane Eaton Member of Seven Oaks, daughter of Robert C. Roberts

Elaine Engst Chief Archivist at Cornell, Project Director of the Robert Trent Jones Collection

Paul Fick Associate Vice-President for Facilities at Colgate

Stan Fisher Member of Seven Oaks

Jerry Freeland Member of the Robert Trent Jones Society

Carolyn Godfrey Editor of the *Mid-York Weekly*

Frank Gundlach Colgate '60, member of the Robert Trent Jones Society

David Hale Colgate '84, Vice President for Finance and Administration at Colgate

Matt Halloran Member of Seven Oaks

James Hansen Auburn University, author of an upcoming book on Robert Trent Jones

Joseph S. Hope Colgate '97, Director of Investments, Colgate, Administrative Liaison for the Seven Oaks Golf Course

Carl Isbell, Jr. Provided family information about his father's efforts in construction of the back nine

Michelle Jacobson Administrative Assistant, Planned Giving at Colgate

Sarah Keen Head of Special Collections, Colgate University Library

Dick Lamb Supervisor of the Town of Madison, retired

Louie Lamb Performed construction work for the back nine of the course

Dave Leonard 1977 N.C.A.A. Tournament Co-Chairman

Todd Lewis Head Mechanic at Seven Oaks maintenance facility

Francesca Livermore Rare Books and Manuscripts Director, Colgate University Library

Polly Mahoney Member of Seven Oaks, daughter of Robert C. Roberts.

Jon McConville Seven Oaks Course Superintendent since 2006

Carrie McFall Secretary, Colgate University Buildings and Grounds

Robert McVaugh Professor of Art and Art History at Colgate

Jim Mlasgar, Jr. Member of Seven Oaks

Irmin and Mary Jane Mody Members of Seven Oaks

Tom and Marilyn Parnell Tom was Seven Oaks Golf Professional, 1963–1974

Phil Perham Associate Director of Planned Giving at Colgate

Arthur Rashap Colgate '58, former member of Seven Oaks, worked on the construction of the front nine as a student at Colgate

Eddie Ray Member of Seven Oaks

Gary Rider Colgate '62, member of Seven Oaks and former head golf coach at Hamilton Central School

Dave Roach Former Colgate University Athletic Director

Laura Rodman Administrative Assistant, Seven Oaks Clubhouse

Roger Rulewich Design Specialist for Robert Trent Jones, Sr.

Bruce Selleck Colgate '71, Interim Provost, Dean of the Faculty, and Director of the Upstate Institute at Colgate

Doug Speer Manager, Seven Oaks Clubhouse

Sue Sutherland Administrative Assistant, *Mid-York Weekly*

Jack and Linda ten Hope Members of Seven Oaks, former managers of the Clubhouse

Dick and Marilyn Upton Members of Seven Oaks

Ed Vantine Colgate '56, member of Seven Oaks

INTRODUCTION

Colgate University's Seven Oaks Golf Course is universally regarded as one of the finest in New York State. Designed by legendary golf course designer Robert Trent Jones, Seven Oaks offers a unique challenge to golfers of all ability levels while also featuring panoramic views of the Colgate campus and the surrounding hillsides.

The history of golf in Hamilton dates back to 1916 when a group of citizens from the Hamilton community and the Colgate faculty proposed the building of a golf course so that all could enjoy the fast-growing sport. Prominent names such as M.S. Read, H.O. Whitnall, E.C. Huntington, S.W. Stradling, O.S. Langworthy, and I. Leland were soon listed as members of the new course "on the hill." Originally known as the Hamilton Golf Club, the name Seven Oaks was adopted when the hillside course was re-configured and expanded in 1928. The new design was created by Thomas Winton, a noted New York City golf course architect.

In the 1930s a proposal to build a new course on portions of the current Seven Oaks location was put into motion through the efforts of William Reid and his good friend and golfing great, Gene Sarazen. On site at the time was a young golf course architect named Robert Trent Jones, who along with his partner Stanley Thompson, designed an 18-hole course.

The idea of a course was later proposed to be a W.P.A. project during the height of the Great Depression. However, final approval was not obtained and the idea languished for a number of years. Prior to World War II, and with the purchase of more land by the University, Mr. Jones was called back to design a new set of plans. However, the attack on Pearl Harbor put the project on hold once again.

Following the war, Bill Reid again contacted Jones to design a nine-hole extension to the "hill course." When additional properties were obtained by the University, the construction of the front nine, and the later addition of a back nine as well, allowed Colgate to finally realize its championship course. Dedications were held for the front nine in 1958 and the back nine in 1965. Seven Oaks had finally become the dream that so many had hoped for.

The course that Robert Trent Jones designed has become the pride of Colgate University and a facility enjoyed by Colgate faculty and staff, community members, alumni, and guests. All can attest to the beauty and difficulty of our "Central New York Gem." Annually listed as one of the top collegiate courses in the nation and one of the top golfing venues in New York State, we can all be proud of the facility offered to us.

Let us travel through the years from 1916 to the present and explore the rich history of golf in Hamilton and Colgate University's Seven Oaks Golf Course.

Scenes of Sevenoaks, Kent, England. The name of the community is written as one word and was the ancestral community of the Colgate family, who lived just outside Sevenoaks at their landed estate known as Filston Farm. In the photos we see the famous seven oak trees and the quaint look of Sevenoaks. Courtesy of the Marian Blain Collection.

ONE THE COLGATE FAMILY AND SEVEN OAKS

The naming of Colgate University and Seven Oaks traces its beginnings back to England during the 1700s. At that time, the Colgate family lived on a landed estate known as Filston Farm. The estate was located in the Shire of Kent, England, and near the community of Sevenoaks. The community today is a quaint tourist location that continues to exhibit the same flavor it possessed during the days when the Colgate family resided there. The name of the community at that time and today is spelled as one word.

Robert, the head of the Colgate family, was a gentleman farmer. He spoke out against the views of King George III and in favor of the French Revolution. These statements were considered by the British government to be treasonous. Receiving word that he was on a list of people to be brought up on charges against the crown, Robert moved his family to the United States and settled near Baltimore, Maryland. This was in 1795.

He and his eldest son, William, soon became partners with Robert Mather in a soap and candle business. The partnership later dissolved, but William was on his way to becoming a master soapmaker.

In 1803 William headed for New York City, where he joined John Slidell & Company, soap and candle manufacturers. He steadily worked his way up to business manager and then, in 1806, founded his own company, William Colgate & Company, on Dutch Street in New York City.

His success with the company and the fortune he made during the War of 1812 allowed him the means to subsidize the budgets of the religious institution in upstate New York that would eventually bear the family name.

The later naming of the Colgate University golf course was a tribute to the Colgate family and the community located near their ancestral home in England.

Sevenoaks, Kent, England. Courtesy of the Marian Blain Collection.

TWO GOLF BEGINS IN HAMILTON

PLANS TO ORGANIZE A GOLF CLUB

A number of men of the village, who have decided that they need a little more outdoor air and exercise, are planning to organize a golf club. This is an admirable idea, and besides it will tend to call men here who during their vacation wish a place to play this popular game. Hamilton ought to afford a good course and a successful club.

Let all interested come to the Citizen's Club, in the Smith Block, Friday evening at 8 o'clock. A discussion of plans will take place and organization effected at that time.

The Hamilton Republican, May 18, 1916

GOLF CLUB MATTERS

Early last summer a movement was started in Hamilton to organize a Golf Club, and with this end in view a meeting was held in the Citizen's Club rooms and the matter talked over. At that time, a committee was appointed to look carefully into the details of the matter and to report upon the advisability and possibility of a Golf Club organization.

The committee consisted of H.H. Hawkins, M.S. Read, A.W. Smith, F.M. Jones and J.J. Taylor. The report of this committee is as follows. The committee has secured an option on a plot of ground belonging to Dr. I.N. Wheeler, located on Payne Street, back of Dr. Wheeler's residence, and secured terms of rental on the same for a term of years. It also had experts here to look over the grounds and to make estimates on the cost of fitting the ground for play and for keeping it in proper condition.

It was found that a membership of at least forty would be necessary for a term of five years at a yearly cost of $20.00 each, in order to safely finance the proposition. After a canvas of the village, it was found that a sufficient number could not be obtained to make the organization safe and it was deemed to hold the matter for present, with the possibility of taking it up again at some future time.

[*The impetus for a course may also have come from knowing that neighboring Norwich had constructed a golf course in 1912.*]

The Hamilton Republican, March 1, 1917

THE WHEELER HOME

The building used for the Seven Oaks Golf Course Clubhouse was known for many years as the Payne home. Built c. 1835 by Deacon Charles C. Payne, the ninth of sixteen sons of Judge Elisha Payne, the home was purchased by

Dr. I.N. Wheeler in 1905. Following the death of Dr. Wheeler, Colgate University acquired the home from his sister in 1954.

Permission was granted from the University to use the Wheeler home for a Clubhouse. Extensive remodeling was done through the efforts of Colgate University, citizens from Hamilton and the surrounding area, and the American Management Association.

The original land area of the Payne Farm had been divided over the years. In the December 14, 1905 edition of the *The Hamilton Republican*, it stated that "Dr. I.N. Wheeler, who recently purchased the Payne Homestead on Payne Street, has just purchased of Mr. John J. Taylor, the 20 acres facing the Payne house, which makes him the owner of the whole of the Payne Farm."

There was once a brick yard and kiln located on the Payne Farm which supplied bricks for a number of structures in Hamilton. The kiln and yard was said to be located in the area of the present 13th tee.

Charles C. Payne, ninth son of Elisha Payne, built the home c. 1835. The home was purchased by Dr. I.N. Wheeler in 1905. Dr. Wheeler helped to establish golf in Hamilton. The Wheeler home would later become the Clubhouse at Seven Oaks. Photo courtesy of the Special Collections and University Archives, Colgate University Libraries.

Information from the *Mid-York Weekly*, May 15, 1958, and *Seeing Hamilton: Your Guide to Village Architecture*, p. 25.

The Wheeler Home in 1909. Built c.1835, large porches graced the structure. The Payne home was purchased by Dr. I.N. Wheeler in 1905. Dr. Wheeler was one of the leaders in establishing a golf course in Hamilton. The barn in the background would become the Pro Shop at Seven Oaks in 1959. Photo courtesy of Special Collections and University Archives, Colgate University Libraries.

Help from the Trustees

The Hamilton Golf Club which was in an embryonic state last spring and which on account of the war or for other reasons did not materialize has received a new lease on life. The Colgate Board of Trustees has given permission to form a golf course on the upper part of the campus, which is up back of the buildings, and this, obviating the expense of grounds, will enable the club to be formed and to maintain itself financially, it is thought.

It is requested that all interested in this subject meet at the Citizen's Club rooms on Tuesday evening next to consider the organization of a Golf Club.

The Hamilton Republican, July 26, 1917

Excellent Prospects for a Golf Club

About forty members have already joined the club and the chairman of the membership committee expects the number to be increased to fifty in the near future.

An expert is expected today and the course will be fitted up immediately. The flags, markers etc., have been ordered and it is expected that the members will be able to become familiar with the course and learn how to handle the sticks during the fall months. One trip around the course and you are a golf enthusiast for life.

The Hamilton Republican, August 9, 1917

Workmen on the Hill

Workmen are engaged in making ready the golf grounds on College Hill. There are to be nine holes and already three of them are about ready for use. Five holes will be ready soon. Markers and flags are here and soon there will be the merry call of "fore."

The Hamilton Republican, August 23, 1917

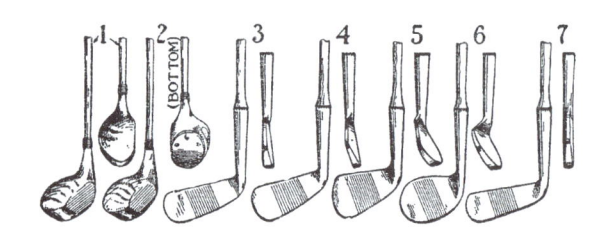

The Original Clubs

Driver	#1 Wood
Brassie	#2 Wood
Spoon	#3 Wood
Driving Iron	#1 Iron
Mid-Iron	#2 Iron
Mid-Mashie	#3 Iron
Mashie Iron	#4 Iron
Mashie	#5 Iron
Spade Mashie	#6 Iron
Mashie Niblick	#7 Iron
Pitching Niblick	#8 Iron
Niblick	#9 Iron

Courtesy of the Jim Ford Collection.

Straight Dope on the New Links

The Hamilton Golf Club has made progress beyond the most optimistic hopes of its promoters. Five of the nine holes are in use and in good condition. The remaining four are laid out and seeded and will be ready for use in the early spring.

The membership has reached and passed the fifty mark, and there is room for more. To join now will only entail the $10.00 initiation fee to play for the remainder of the season.

There are few golf links in the country located as beautifully as ours. From the 4th tee, west to the quarry, one has a view of the valley and surrounding hills that begs description. Why, the first time Squire Burke played the course he found three shamrocks and hasn't missed a day since!

The Hamilton Republican, September 27, 1917

Golf Club Members

The following is a list of the Charter Members of the Hamilton Golf Club:

M.S. Read, H.H. Hawkins, H.O. Whitnall, J.J. Feeley, R.G. Ingraham, E.C. Huntington, F.W. Piotrow, I.N. Wheeler, W.L. Burke, F.M. Jones, W.H. Hixon, F.A. Starratt, J.D. MacQueen, H.C. Williamson, A.P. Brigham, F.G. Mott, E.H. Stone, S.W. Stradling, A.N. Smith, W.T. Elmore, C.J. Griswold, W. Bardeen, F.H. Allen, A.J. Newton, A.S. Sheldon, G.W. Berry, H.R. Berry, J.J. Taylor, T.B. Bell, F.N. Tompkins, J.W. Farrar, B. Lynch, F.L. Shepardson, C.M. Coe, O.S. Langworthy, D.F. Estes, H.P. Wells, E.W. Goodhue, E.B. Bryan, W.H. Allison, R.W. Craine, N.D. VanSlyke, I. Leland, C.S. Orvis, W.F. Reil, W.O. Stearns, J.F. Vichert, G.F. Barford, F.C. Ewart, J.B. Anderson, W.H. Hoerner, W.M. Chester.

Mr. James Feeley is chairman of the Membership Committee and will gladly receive application for membership from many more Hamiltonians.

The Hamilton Republican, July 11, 1918

Men and Women Represented

The local golf links are becoming more popular daily. Women frequent the course almost as much as men. Associated as it is with the big outdoors, the game is rapidly winning additional enthusiasts. Just at present there is a demand for caddies, especially among those who wish to practice driving.

The Hamilton Republican, June 19, 1919

The New Mower

The local golf club has been in need of a horse lawn mower for use on its course and learning of this need several generous guests of the University during Commencement Week contributed to a fund of $300 for this purpose. This will supply a long felt want and will help greatly to put the course in much better condition.

The Hamilton Republican, June 26, 1919

Golf Club Plans Handicap Tournament

Members of the Hamilton Golf Club are preparing for the first tournament to be staged on the local grounds. First award in the tournament will be possession of the Jerome Handicap Golf Tournament Cup until the date of the succeeding tournament. This cup is a handsome silver trophy presented to the local golf club by Mr. William Travers Jerome, Jr., of New York City.

Mr. Jerome is a member of the Board of Trustees of the University. During his visit to Hamilton at Commencement time he became much interested in the local golf club. This interest has recently found expression in the donation of two costly trophy cups, the Jerome Handicap Cup and the College Interfraternity Cup.

The handicap tournament is open to every member of the club. Each player should provide himself with score cards (these are to be found in the "Clubhouse"—one time Dr. Read's garage) and carefully keep his score on each round of play. In this way fair handicaps can be assigned.

The Hamilton Republican, August 21, 1919

Scorecard for the Hamilton Golf Club. This was the first course "on the hill" and featured 2,012 yards for nine holes. You played the nine again for an 18-hole score. The total yardage would then have been 4,024 yards. Photo courtesy of Special Collections and University Archives, Colgate University Libraries.

Golfing at the Hamilton Golf Club c.1920. Dr. Alton is in knickers and Fred Jones has a bow tie. Photo courtesy of Special Collections and University Archives, Colgate University Libraries.

EARLY ROUNDS—CHILLY TEMPERATURES

The chilly breezes have not affected the ardor of the local golf enthusiasts. Many rounds have already been played and the links is gaining greater popularity. Many local people have now solved the mysteries behind such terms as, "fore," "stymie," and "niblick." A round in the 70s is the ambition of more than one devotee.

The Hamilton Republican, April 29, 1920

IMPROVEMENTS TO THE COURSE

The golf links are growing in popularity. Many followers of the sport are availing themselves of the opportunities offered by the splendid course on the hill. Arrangements have been made for the services of an expert who will come here soon to make improvements on the course. New bunkers will be added and attention will be given to the fairways and greens. The handicap championship tournament will be played again this year.

The Hamilton Republican, June 20, 1920

SOME SERIOUS GOLFING

Some very serious golf has been played on the local links the past week. Mr. Charles DeAngelis and Mr. Whitney Shepardson laid down a record by playing 414 holes in one week. This is an average of 69 holes per day for six days. On this nine-hole course they went around between seven and eight times per day. They lost but two balls during the week.

The Hamilton Republican, August 19, 1920

Hamilton Golf Course Fees

Numerous inquiries have been made regarding the privileges of the Hamilton Golf Course to non-residents and to others who do not hold a season membership card. The course is now in such condition that many from out of town are attracted to it.

Daily, weekly, and monthly membership cards may be obtained upon the grounds at the following rates:
- Daily $ .50
- Weekly $2.00
- Monthly $5.00

The Hamilton Republican, June 29, 1922

Accident at the Course

Dr. Isaiah N. Wheeler was quite badly injured on the Colgate University golf links about noon on Monday. Dr. Wheeler had been playing golf with his brother, Dr. William Wheeler, and his brother-in-law, John Murphy, and were driven into the shelter of a lumber pile during a thunderstorm. They had been under the protection of the lumber pile only a few minutes when the wind blew it over onto them. Dr. Wheeler was in the act of looking at his watch and was unable to heed the warning cries of his companions who jumped to safety.

Dr. Wheeler was buried beneath the pile and before he could be extricated he was in a critical condition. He was unconscious when he was removed to his home on Payne Street, remaining in this condition for several hours. His back and both legs were badly injured. He also received bruises on the head.

Considering the weight and quantity of lumber that fell on him it is a wonder that he was not killed. John Murphy was caught in the falling pile but was not badly injured. Dr. William Wheeler escaped unhurt.

The Hamilton Republican, August 3, 1922

An Early Course Record

Question has arisen as to low score on the local golf links. An inquiry recently resulted in disclosing the fact that Mr. Whitney Shepardson has covered the course in 40. As far as can be ascertained, this record has never been lowered. Mr. Charles DeAngelis, of Utica, is a close rival with a score of 41.

The Hamilton Republican, August 26, 1922

Bill Reid Initiates Plans for a Course

Mr. Thomas Winton of New York City has been in Hamilton for the past few days making a layout and estimate for an eighteen-hole golf course. Although there will probably be a nine-hole course here for a few years, we may look forward to an eighteen-hole course sometime in the future.

[*This plan did not move forward but Winton was called back the next year to modify the original golf course and lay out six new holes.*]

The Hamilton Republican, May 6, 1926

Golfing attire for 1922.
The Hamilton Republican, August 17, 1922

A New Golf Course

It was announced Monday by Graduate Manager William A. Reid, Secretary of the Colgate University Alumni Athletic Council, that the Council has appropriated the sum of $5,000 to be turned over to the Colgate Alumni Fund. The contribution is designed for the express purpose of initiating a movement for the building of a new golf course on the recently acquired property immediately south of the campus.

This land consists of two farms known as the Dart and Dunster properties. The Dart Farm was given to the University by George W. Cobb, President of the Alumni Corporation. The Dunster Farm, on which is located the original house in which the "13" founders of Colgate University met on September 24, 1819, was acquired by the University through the generosity of an alumnus whose name is for the present withheld.

Raymond E. Brooks, Executive Secretary of the Colgate University Alumni Corporation, stated today that a sufficient sum of money has been subscribed to warrant the breaking of ground at once for a new course.

[*The Dart Farm, of nearly 150 acres, was given to the University in 1920. Bill Reid's full name was William Alonzo Reid.*]

The Hamilton Republican, June 16, 1927

An early photo of William A. Reid. Bill Reid was instrumental in the push for our present Seven Oaks Golf Course. Photo courtesy of Special Collections and University Archives, Colgate University Libraries.

Golf Architect Is Hired

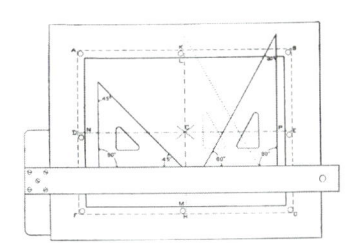

Mr. Thomas Winton, golf architect of New York City, has been in Hamilton for a few days this week laying out the six holes on the new golf course and getting the work of building these holes started.

Mr. Winton has laid out many courses in various parts of the country, and is considered an expert in this kind of work. The new links are being laid out on the Dart and Dunster Farms and promises to be a very fine course.

[*A few of the other courses designed by Thomas Winton included Woods Hole Golf Club, Mount Kisco Country Club, Corning Country Club, Saxon Woods Golf Club, Hopewell Valley Golf Club, Mill River Country Club, and the Westport Golf Club.*]

The Hamilton Republican, June 30, 1927

Progress on the New Course

The new nine-hole golf course which has been under construction during the past few months will be opened sometime next year. The course will be known as the Colgate Golf Course and will be maintained by the University. The cost for the course is estimated to be around $15,000 which has been contributed by the Colgate Athletic Association and the Colgate Alumni.

Mr. Thomas Winton of New York City is the architect for the new course and he has made frequent trips to Hamilton to supervise the work. Dr. I.N. Wheeler, Chairman of the Green Committee, who has been in charge of the old course for the past three years, has been in charge of the construction of the new course. Dr. Wheeler has done more for golf in Hamilton than any other person. He has given the present course his constant attention and has assisted in a financial way to put the course in its present condition.

The course will be a little over 3,000 yards long with several difficult holes. Three of the holes will be located on the present course. The greens are to be much larger than the present ones and the holes much longer.

Richard "Dick" Haley with his crew has been working since July laying out the fairways and greens so that the course may be open for play next year. A new feature of the course is that there will be water for each of the greens.

The Hamilton Republican, September 22, 1927

OTHER ARCHITECTS WERE CONSIDERED

Thomas Winton, of New York City, received the job for the new Seven Oaks course "on the hill." However, he was not the only golf architect contacted for the work. Others included Walter J. Travis and Donald Ross, (who both indicated by letters to Colgate that they were too busy at the time), H.F. Andrews, Maurice J. McCarthy (who had been informed of the project by A.G. Spalding & Bros.), Seymour Dunn, William Tucker & Son and Seth Raynor.

Winton estimated that the cost of the project would be $25,000 for nine holes and $55,000 for eighteen. Colgate's accounting of the cost at "approximately" $21,000 for the first nine came very close to his estimate. Winton's architectural fee was listed as $1,500.

From the Colgate University Archives: sports articles

BILL REID AND "DOC" WHEELER ARE BUSY

The Athletic Council has taken over the management of both the old and new courses. Both will be maintained during the year 1928. The care of the new course will not interfere with play on the old nine holes. Through the kindness of Dr. Cutten, President of the University, the barn on the Olmstead property will be at the disposal of the Athletic Council. The dues for membership for the year 1928 are as follows:

- Resident (Individual) $25.00
- Resident (Family) $35.00
- Resident (Individual Lady) $15.00
- Resident (Junior Ages 14–20) $10.00
- Non-Resident (Individual) $15.00
- Non-Resident (Family) $25.00
- Green fees will be $1.00

The Hamilton Republican, May 17, 1928

GOLF COURSE NEARLY COMPLETED

Soon the conversation from caddies and the crack of determined niblicks will be heard from the new Seven Oaks Golf Course, consisting of nine holes and a total yardage of 3003 yards.

Named for the English ancestral home of the Colgate family, this new course promises to be a rendezvous of recreation for the golfers of this area.

It was designed by Thomas Winton, of New York City, and will cost approximately $21,000. The new course will have three holes on the old University course and six holes on the Dunn and Dunster farms. It crosses a ravine that is from four to twenty feet deep four times, and the elevation of 2,000 feet at this point enables one to see for miles across the beautiful Chenango Valley.

William A. Reid was given full charge of the new course in May. Dr. I.N. Wheeler has been in charge of the construction. The new course will be for the use of members of the Seven Oaks Golf Club, which will be supervised by the Colgate Athletic Council, and will be operated in conjunction with the Colgate Inn for the benefit of visitors to Hamilton.

Yardage for the new course is as follows:

HOLE	YARDAGE	PAR
One	367	4
Two	405	4
Three	349	4
Four	456	5
Five	126	3
Six	329	4
Seven	344	4
Eight	200	3
Nine	427	4

TOTAL YARDAGE 3003
PAR 35
18-HOLE COURSE 6006 yards, par 70

[*During the construction of the new course, the Athletic Council, formed in 1928, decided on the name of Seven Oaks for the course instead of the Colgate Golf Club. Golf Club and Golf Course were both used in articles.*]

The Hamilton Republican, July 26, 1928

OPENING OF THE GOLF CLUB

To all lovers of golf, next Monday, August 13th will be the gala day of the season, when the Seven Oaks Golf Club will hold the official opening of the new golf course. The management of the new golf club announces that they have arranged as a special feature, a foursome of Sherrill Sherman, one of the best golfers in New York State and leading player of the Yahnundasis Golf Club of Utica, and Dick Hatfield, Miles Hutchinson, and W.P. Doolittle. These players are the premier amateurs of the Yahnundasis Golf Club. This foursome will play two rounds starting at 2 p.m. At 5 p.m. the lady membership of the club will serve refreshments at the Caddy House.

The officials of the Seven Oaks Golf Club are to be commended for bringing such a remarkable foursome to help in dedicating this new course and every member of the club should show their appreciation toward the officials by being present on this date.

The Hamilton Republican, August 9, 1928

EARLY TERMS OF THE GAME

The Track	The route that the golf course takes
Front Nine	The first nine holes of the course
Back Nine	The last nine holes of the course
Green Fee	The charge for playing the course
Teeing Ground	The area at the beginning of each hole to hit the ball from
Mulligan	An extra shot, usually taken on the first tee
Foursome	A group of four players enjoying a round together
Caddie	A person hired to carry your bag and to give advice about the course.
Fairway	The closely mowed area of a golf hole that follows the route of the track
Rough	An area allowed to grow in length along each side of the fairway
Dogleg	A left or right-hand turn on the fairway
Casual Water	Water that has accumulated in the playing area from storms or construction projects
Slice	The ball is heading to the right from the intended line of flight
Hook	The ball is heading to the left from the intended line of flight
Foot Wedge	Tapping the ball with your foot to get a better lie
Fore	The word you yell to warn other players on the course of your errant shot
Divot	The dirt and sod that is displaced on your shot
Trap	An area, usually of sand, where an errant shot might land
Sandy	Getting out of the sand trap and converting your putt in two strokes
Green	The tightly mowed area where the flagstick is located and the hole ends
Putter	The club used to finish the hole when on the green
Flagstick	The marker on the green which indicates where the cup is located
Stymie	To block an opponent's ball on the green with your own ball
Par	The number of strokes in which you are supposed to be able to complete the hole
Birdie	Scoring one stroke under par for a hole
Eagle	Scoring two strokes under par for a hole
Albatross	Scoring three strokes under par for a hole
Bogey	Scoring one stroke over the par for a hole
Snowman	Scoring an eight on a hole
Handicap	The number of shots that you are given to compensate for the difference in playing ability among golfers
Pro Shop	An area to register to play the course and to buy golf merchandise
Greenkeeper	The person in charge of the golfing area; tees, fairways, rough, bunkers and greens
19th Hole	The name for the Clubhouse. A place to relax after a round of golf

Courtesy of the Jim Ford Collection.

Mehler Breaks Record

Nick Mehler, Captain of the Colgate football team two years ago, returned to Hamilton yesterday and broke the course record at the Seven Oaks Golf Club. Mehler played his rounds with "Bill" Reid and "Denny" Hooper. His score is as follows:

    1st round   5-5-4-5-3-4-4-4-4 = 38
    2nd round 4-5-4-4-3-3-4-4-5 = 36
    Total = 74

This score is better than that made by Sherrill Sherman of Utica.

[*"Denny" Hooper was the Manager of the Colgate Inn at that time.*]

The Hamilton Republican, September 6, 1928

Bill Reid Wins Cup

The first annual tournament of the Seven Oaks Golf Club was ended Saturday afternoon when W.A. "Bill" Reid defeated Wesley Bacon one up in the championship flight. The match was close throughout and was not won until the final putt.

The second flight was won by W.L. Burke over Dr. I.N. Wheeler, two up. The ladies championship was won by Prudence Hawkins from Mrs. H.O. Whitnall.

The Hamilton Republican, September 13, 1928

James Dalgety Named Seven Oaks Pro

Hamilton golfers have the opportunity to improve their golf game with the appointment of the first golf professional, last Monday. "Jimmy" Dalgety, assistant professional at the Yahnundasis Golf Club in Utica, has been named mentor at the Seven Oaks Golf Club and will assume his duties on the new course, beginning next April. Throughout the winter, he will be busy organizing a golf school at Colgate with the aid of "Jack" Ginster, captain of the team.

Mr. Dalgety came from Scotland about three years ago and has already acquired a fine reputation in the golfing circles of Central New York State. He is an apt student of the game and in addition to being an excellent teacher; he is an expert fashioner of golf clubs.

A specially equipped portion of the spacious Huntington Gymnasium will be given over to the golf school which will open on December 8th. The upper west wing of the building will be utilized by the school which will have nets installed and "putting" for the winter practice. The school will be open to all students, alumni and Hamilton townspeople at a reasonable fee.

Early photo of James M. Dalgety, a native of Carnoustie, Scotland, and the first "Golf Professional" at Colgate. Photo courtesy of Special Collections and University Archives, Colgate University Libraries.

[*Dalgety was an assistant to Pete Robinson at the Yahnundasis in 1927–28. His full name was James Myles Dalgety. Golf would be introduced as an intramural program to the Colgate students by Dalgety in 1930.*]

The Hamilton Republican, October 18, 1928

Narrow Escape at the Course

George Marshall had a narrow escape from being crushed soon after he went to work on the Seven Oaks Golf Course yesterday morning. The big rocks are being dynamited and Mr. Marshall and Peter McCormick were drawing away the broken stone. A big stone, which would weigh more than half a ton, rolled onto Mr. Marshall, pinning one of his legs beneath it. Owing to the soft ground, no bones were broken. He will be confined to the house for some time.

The Hamilton Republican, October 25, 1928

Dalgety and the Caddy House

Hamilton is getting its first golf weather and "Jimmy" Dalgety, the new "pro," is now on the job at the course. Through the efforts of Henry Berry, local insurance man, the Seven Oaks Golf Club has secured burglary insurance in the amount of $3,000 to cover the supplies of the Golf Professional at the Caddy House.

The Caddy House is located at the extreme south end of the Colgate campus and this insurance assures apprehension and punishment to pilferers.

The Hamilton Republican, April 25, 1929

Lloyd Jordan Gets First Hole-in-One

Last Friday afternoon, Lloyd Jordan, Colgate's basketball coach and assistant football coach, laid claim to the honor of being the first golfer to score a hole-in-one on the Seven Oaks Golf Course.

Jordan was playing in a foursome consisting of D.D. Hooper, Manager of the Colgate Inn, former District Attorney W.L. Burke and James Dalgety, local professional. The feat took place on the short fifth hole where Jordan took an iron and landed the ball about fifteen feet from the pin and it rolled down and into the cup.

"Denny" Hooper, shooting just before Jordan, hit the pin and barely missed a coveted hole-in-one.

The Hamilton Republican, June 20, 1929

Local Man Breaks Golf Course Record

William H. "Stub" Mooney now holds the honors of the Seven Oaks Golf Course by virtue of his playing last Tuesday afternoon when he played nine holes with a score of 34. This is the first time that the par of the course, which is 35, has ever been broken.

"Stub" was playing in a threesome with Dr. I.N. Wheeler and Warren Alton. His score was as follows: 5, 4, 3, 4, 3, 5, 4, 2, 4—34. This is a real accomplishment for a local man when we consider that some of the best professional golfers in Central New York have played the course and have failed to get such a low score on nine holes.

The Hamilton Republican, July 18, 1929

REID WINS FOR A SECOND YEAR

William A. "Bill" Reid was the winner of the second annual tournament of the Seven Oaks Golf Club after having defeated Prof. F.M. Jones, two up, in the finals. The ladies championship was won by Kathryn Williams, who defeated Mrs. H.O. Whitnall. The tournament was run by James Dalgety, local "pro."

The Hamilton Republican, September 5, 1929

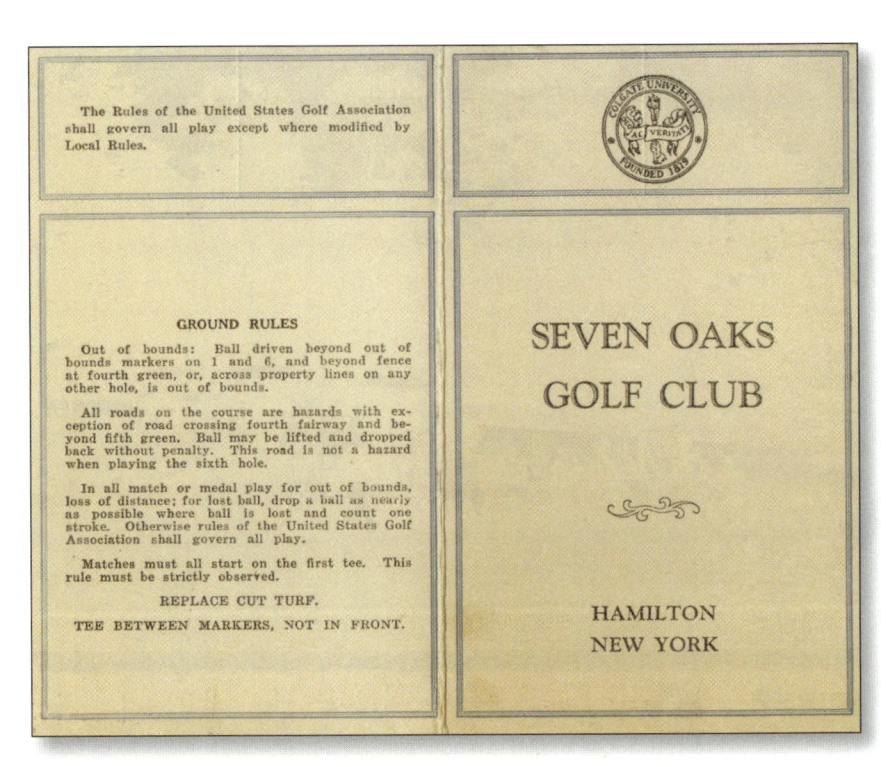

Scorecard from the Seven Oaks course "on the hill." We see that the total yardage had been increased from the 3,003 yards stated in the July 26, 1928, article to 3,007 yards. Photo courtesy of Special Collections and University Archives, Colgate University Libraries.

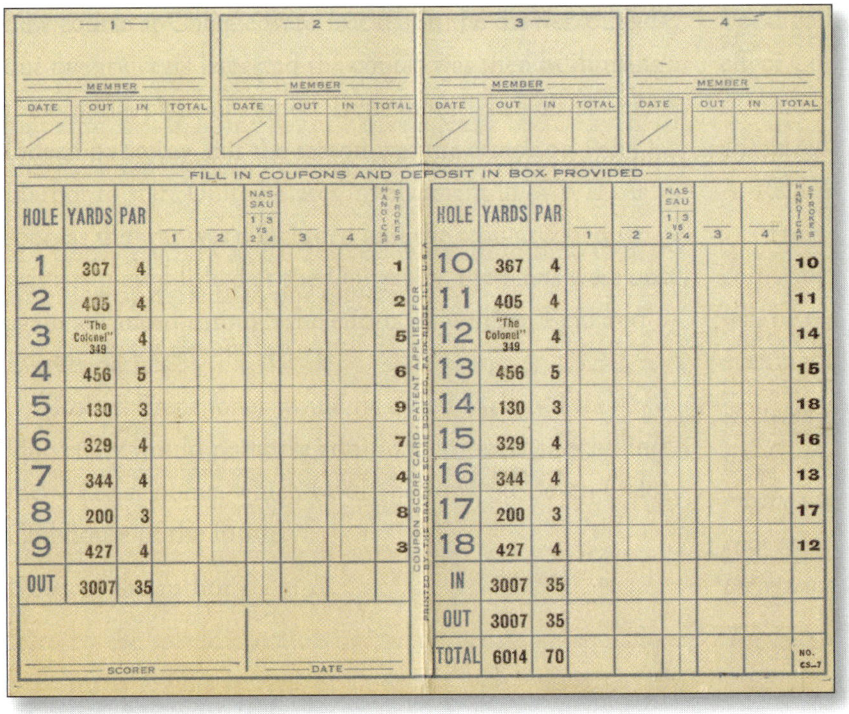

When Pa Comes Homes in the Fall

"Who's the stranger, mother dear?
Look! He knows us—ain't that queer?"
"Hush, my own, don't talk so wild;
He's your father dearest child."
"He's my father? No such thing!
Father died away last spring."
"Father didn't die you bub!
Father joined a golfing club.
But they've closed the club, so he
Has no place to go, you see—
No place left for him to roam—
That is why he's coming home.
Kiss him; he won't bite you, child;
All them golfing guys look wild."
—Author unknown

The Hamilton Republican, November 14, 1929

In Memory of Dr. Read

Last week there was placed on the Seven Oaks Golf Course, near the first tee, a bronze tablet to the memory of Dr. Melbourne S. Read. On it are the following words:

> No. 1—"Pioneer"
> In Honor of Melbourne S. Read,
> who had the vision,
> courage and faith
> to pioneer golf at
> Colgate in 1917.
>
> Let's play the game
> as he would have us,
> always as gentlemen.

Dr. Read took a great interest in the golf course from its beginning and the inscription on the bronze tablet is very appropriate for the man in whose memory it was erected.

[*There was also a hole named for Colonel Austen Colgate, long-time Treasurer of Colgate University. It was appropriately named "The Colonel."*]

The Hamilton Republican, September 25, 1930

Golfing at the Colgate Inn

The Colgate Inn has recently installed in the Sports Room of the Inn, downstairs under the lobby, a nine-hole indoor golf course, of the Witt construction. This is the third of three such courses outside of New York City, the others being in Albany and Syracuse.

The walls of the room have been artistically decorated with landscape views, and at the entrance is a caddy house and fountain. James Dalgety, the Seven Oaks Professional, will officiate here also. The official opening of the course is to be sometime next week.

The Hamilton Republican, October 30, 1930

Wheeler's Hole-in-One

Dr. I.N. Wheeler, Hamilton golf enthusiast, entered golfdom's hall of fame Tuesday afternoon when he made a hole-in-one on the fifth hole of the Seven Oaks Golf Course, Hamilton. Dr. Wheeler was playing the round with "Stub" Mooney, who verified the shot. Two other golfers who were playing nearby were also called to witness the feat.

Some time ago Dr. Wheeler made the sixth hole in two, which has not been accomplished by anyone else on this course, according to existing records.

Lloyd Jordan scored a hole-in-one on the fifth a year ago last summer, and Frank Howe, Buffalo, a former Colgate student, achieved this feat soon after Jordan's accomplishment.

Otsego Farmer and Republican, October 2, 1931

Paging Dr. Wheeler!!

Paging Dr. Wheeler and the rest of our Hamiltonians in sunny Florida—Hear Ye!! "Stub" Mooney and Fred Graves played a round of golf on January 10th and report the Seven Oaks Course in excellent condition. Harry Cookus, the genial Manager of the Colgate Inn, is about to advertise Hamilton as a place where skating can be enjoyed in the morning and golf and tennis in the afternoon.

[*In 1930 Harry Cookus became Manager of the Colgate Inn. Dennis Hooper left Hamilton for a position in New York City.*]

The Hamilton Republican, January 14, 1932

Finicky Cow Snubs Golf Balls

Hamilton—Lant Gilmartin's cow Susie today refused to eat any more golf balls. For five years Susie has leaned hungrily against the fence of her pasture which adjoins the Seven Oaks Golf Course, waiting for a sliced drive. Then Susie has eaten the golf ball as if it were an apple.

But today, perhaps because it is the 13th, Susie sniffed disdainfully at a ball and returned to eating grass. "Maybe she's got a little touch of indigestion," said Lant. "I can't believe she's getting finicky in her old age."

[*Lant Gilmartin was the Director of University Grounds at Colgate for many years.*]

Binghamton Press, September 13, 1932

THREE: GENE SARAZEN, ROBERT TRENT JONES, AND A GOLF COURSE CONTROVERSY

SARAZEN WILL DESIGN NEW COLGATE COURSE

Gene Sarazen, former British and American Open title holder, announced in a talk before the Colgate student body in the Memorial Chapel Wednesday morning, that he will make the new 18-hole golf course to be started here in the spring his own home course and that it will be constructed so as to carry out his ideas in every detail concerning an "ideal" course. The reason for Sarazen's visit to Hamilton was a mystery until he made the announcement.

Mr. Sarazen came to Hamilton by airplane and train Tuesday after finishing play in the Miami Open on Sunday. He spent most of Tuesday afternoon in conference with William A. Reid, graduate manager of athletics, and Stanley Thompson and Robert Trent Jones, golf architects, and in looking over the 147-acre tract where the course is to be built.

Sarazen revealed that for years he has hoped to build a course exactly the way he wanted it. After looking over the Colgate acreage he reached the conclusion that it was just the type of tract that would make it possible for him to construct a course of championship caliber. When he made the announcement to the students, he was met with an enthusiastic ovation.

Mr. Sarazen was given a dinner at the Colgate Inn Tuesday night, hosted by President George B. Cutten. In attendance were the architects, prominent Hamilton businessmen, and Mr. Reid. Mr. Sarazen and Bill Reid have been friends for several years.

Sarazen's plan is to make the course challenging for professionals and top-notch amateurs, yet fair enough for the ordinary player. He intends to return to Hamilton in the spring to work out his ideas about how all the holes should be laid out and finally supervise all details so that the course will be ready to open in 1935. He plans to hit out hundreds of balls to judge placement of natural hazards and the location of traps.

The tract of land on which the course is to be built is 147 acres in extent and owned by the University. It has been known as the Dunn Farm. It is bounded by Hamilton Street on the south, Spring Street on the east, Payne Street on the north and by the land back of University Avenue on the west. Payne's Creek flows through one end of it and there is another stream which runs down from Bonney Hill and crosses the property. The terrain is rolling, without steep hills but with enough slopes to make it interesting as a course.

Reid and Sarazen left for New York City Wednesday afternoon. The complete details of the course are yet to be worked out but announcements will be made at various times as progress is made.

[*The architectural firm was known as Thompson, Jones & Company, with offices in Toronto and New York City. Thompson was a Canadian architect. Jones left this company and began his own firm in 1938. In the original plans for the course, as designed by Robert Trent Jones and incorporating the ideas of Gene Sarazen, the layout would not extend to the north side of Payne Street. That property would be put into plans at a later date. The Dunn Farm had been purchased by Colgate in 1933 from Florence C. Dunn. Mr. Dennison Rogers was the surveyor of the land purchased by Colgate.*]

The Hamilton Republican, January 11, 1934

A Design for a Diamond Ring

A story that has been widely circulated is that Robert Trent Jones used the money from his original design for the Colgate golf course to buy a diamond ring for his wife. Jones first designed the Colgate course in 1934, the same year that he married the former Ione Tefft Davis of Montclair, New Jersey.

Ms. Davis' father did not initially approve of Jones. Mr. Davis thought that his daughter could do better than to marry a golf course designer. He finally consented to the marriage after Jones had proven that his golf course designs could generate substantial money, even during the years of the Great Depression.

The dates of our original course design and the marriage of Jones on May 11, 1934, at St. Lukes Episcopal Church in Montclair indicate that our story is a true one. From the obituary of Robert Trent Jones and notes of the author.

Hoping for Assistance

During the following months, Bill Reid and Gene Sarazen hoped for assistance from the federal government in the form of a W.P.A. (Works Progress Administration) project. This seemed to be the best avenue with which to build the proposed golf course due to limited funding opportunities during the Great Depression from other sources.

Notes of the author

Other Types of Hazards

As we anxiously hear of a new course to be laid out by Gene Sarazen, we relate that in its early stages, our Seven Oaks course "on the hill" had curious hazards which consisted of long grass, thorn bushes, and a herd of 30 cows. You often yelled "fore" in vain.

Colgate Maroon, January 12, 1934

Damages to the Caddy House

A terrific storm took the front porch and a part of the roof of the Caddy House on the Seven Oaks Golf Course. The porch and roof were blown onto the 9th green.

Colgate Maroon, May 11, 1934

Background to the Sarazen Connection

A letter from William Reid to George W. Cobb
August 22, 1934

I trust you will forgive me for the tardy reply subsequent to the very fine chat I had the other day with Robert Trent Jones, golf architect. I asked Jones to come and see you and tell you about this golf course project in Hamilton.

    I believe there are great possibilities in this project with proper handling. I would like to give you somewhat of a history as to how this all happened. I was invited to a dinner in 1932 by Grantland Rice and the other guests included Alec Morrison, golf writer, and Gene Sarazen. At that time Sarazen said that he intended to build his idea of an ideal golf course when the opportunity presented itself. He hoped to have the course in the north so as not to conflict with Augusta National. Jokingly, I remarked to Sarazen that if he ever became serious on that idea to come to Colgate and pay us a visit for we had the land for such an ideal layout.

    A little while later, the Robert Trent Jones that paid you a visit, being a golf architect partner of Stanley Thompson, happened into Hamilton and following an invitation by Dr. Huntington, looked over our land. Thompson and Jones were naturally very closely associated with Sarazen and conveyed to him this possibility. We then talked it over in a general way and Sarazen paid us a visit, expressing the hope that he would like to build the course here. The architects are enthused and so is Sarazen.

Alexander's Hole-in-One

Lee Alexander, Colgate student and pitcher on the freshman baseball team, recorded a hole-in-one on the 9th hole recently.

The Hamilton Republican, September 20, 1934

Striking Caddies Pelt the Players

Caddies at the Seven Oaks Golf Course at Colgate University, Hamilton, went on strike Wednesday during a match with the Canasawacta Club, of Norwich, and during the "rioting" that followed, Robert Roberts, local publisher, was struck by a stone thrown by one of the strikers. Some of the caddies who remained at work were pelted with green apples and stones.

    The trouble started when James Dalgety, Professional, asked the Norwich players to bring nine caddies because of the shortage of bag carriers at Seven Oaks. The Hamilton caddies resented this and struck immediately. Gathering near trees, they booed the players and especially the caddies from Norwich, and the three local caddies who refused to strike.

The Cooperstown Glimmerglass Daily,
August 1, 1935

More About the Caddie Strike

More information has now been learned concerning the caddy strike at Seven Oaks. In addition to the resentment of the Norwich caddies showing up and cutting into their work, the caddies demanded the following: 80 cents per man for carrying double, the chance to play the course two days a week and permission to have impromptu football and softball games behind the Caddy House when not working.

Most of the trouble started when the caddies learned of the Norwich caddies arriving. The Hamilton caddies resented this because it eliminated the chances of them carrying double and earning more money. The heckling and throwing of rocks and apples continued throughout the match. The hollering from the striking caddies was said to be heard all the way down to Huntington Gymnasium.

[*It is odd that the number of striking caddies was 13, usually a lucky number for Colgate. The other oddity is that we would assume that some of the striking caddies were members of or soon to be members of the new Hamilton High School golf team which was formed c.1935.*]

The Hamilton Republican, August 1, 1935

W.P.A. Plans 18-Hole Course Here

Mayor William A. Reid this week received notification from Thomas B. Bergan, of Utica, District W.P.A. Director, that the Works Progress Administration project for an 18-hole municipal golf course in Hamilton has been approved, it was announced Wednesday. Actual allocation of the money, however, will be withheld until pending financial matters have been adjusted, it was stated.

Two days before the November 5 elections it was unofficially reported in an Associated Press story from Albany that Lester W. Herzog, upstate W.P.A. administrator, had approved the expenditure of $97,276 for the course.

Mayor Reid said he could not comment officially on the amount of money involved, because the exact funds have not been decided upon. The letter sent by Bergan, Director of W.P.A. District 6, which includes Madison County, has been the only word received here, the Mayor said.

According to plans for the proposed project, the 18-hole course will be laid out on the land to the west of the Colgate campus formerly known as the Dunn Farm. According to inside information the course will be one of the best in the country.

[*It was called a municipal golf course because William Reid had asked the University to deed the former Dunn Farm property over to the village. The University would then assume a financial sponsorship of the course. After the completion of the course, the village, in the words of Mr. Reid, would prefer to turn the course over to the University for maintenance and supervision.*]

From notes of the Colgate Athletic Council Meeting, October 5, 1935, and the *The Hamilton Republican,* November 14, 1935

The Course Sparks a Controversy

To the editor of the *Hamilton Republican*:
The statement in your paper of last week concerning an "approved" expenditure of approximately $100,000 of Government money for a "municipal golf course" at Hamilton seems to me to suggest some important ques-

tions to which the people of the Village should know the answer before the Village is committed to such a project.

First, by what facts or conditions or reasoning can it be shown that such a project is a proper one for the Village to undertake? Is there an impelling necessity for a course? It is suggested that "the Village" will benefit from such a project by being able to "boast" about it. Many, and probably most of the taxpayers of the Village will have neither time nor money to play golf. Are they to get their "benefit" solely by "boasting" about a course used by others?

Secondly, will the Village be able to maintain such a course without a tax on the people of the Village? Can it be guaranteed that the taxpayers will never be required to be taxed for this purpose?

Thirdly, is the Government to provide the entire cost of construction of the course? If not, where is the Village to get the rest of the money?

Fourthly, is the money to be provided by the Government to be a GIFT to the Village? Or, will it have to be repaid by the Village?

Fifthly, we have heard much complaint about WASTE OF PUBLIC FUNDS and about BALANCING THE BUDGET. If we participate in a raid on the public treasury in order to get something to "boast" about, we certainly cannot justly complain about pouring out public money elsewhere.

I would like to see the Village of Hamilton keep their hands clean in this matter. Then and only then, can we complain about profligate spending by the Government, and advocate balancing the budget.

J. Melbourne Shortliffe
Hamilton, November 20, 1935

The Hamilton Republican, November 21, 1935

SHORTLIFFE WRITES AGAIN

To the editor of the *Hamilton Republican:*
Many persons have expressed approval of the questions concerning a municipal golf course published under my name in your paper three weeks ago. No answer, however, has been given to the taxpayers of the Village to any of those questions.

I have searched the minutes of the Village Board from the beginning of 1935 to the present. In all of the minutes I have found only one motion referring to a golf course. On May 10th an authorization was made for the Mayor to make application to the Government for funds for a municipal golf course in Hamilton.

I found one other item in the record that may be interpreted as relating to a municipal golf course. That is a resolution adopted that "agrees to accept, the gift by deed," of the land on which is to be constructed the golf course.

It appears that this announced project is a deep, dark secret. As such, it stands in marked contrast to other important projects for Hamilton such as sewers and the new State road. In those cases, the people have been given the essential facts of each project, including what was to be done and the costs. With the golf course project, the people have not been consulted. They are merely told that the project is to be done. Is this an example of responsible and responsive government?

J. Melbourne Shortliffe
December 11, 1935

The Hamilton Republican, December 11, 1935

Inquiring of the Man on the Street

Mr. Editor:

When I read Mayor Reid's announcement that Hamilton was to have a Municipal Golf Course, my desire was to shed more light on the subject, and I immediately set out to find it. So I asked six people about the proposed project.

1 No. 1. The first man I interviewed wanted more light too. He replied that he knew little about the matter; and that Hamilton had no more use for a golf course than a cat has for two tails.

2 No. 2. Said that he knew nothing about it and cared nothing; that the Board had their plans made and would do as they pleased regardless of what the people said.

3 No. 3. A leading citizen simply declared his ignorance of the subject and his belief that few people knew anything about the proposition.

4 No. 4. Understood the plan but was against it, because it seemed to him "underhanded."

5 No. 5. A man who has had much to do with Village affairs stated that he knew nothing of the project.

6 No. 6. I next interviewed a member of the Board. He explained the plan so clearly in ten minutes that I was changed from an opponent to a defender of the undertaking.

More light on the subject is what the people want. The Board can shed that light and greatly strengthen its hold on the confidence of the people.

     S.B. Leary

The Hamilton Republican, December 19, 1935

Concerning the Municipal Golf Course

Following are the essential facts regarding the 18-hole municipal golf course for Hamilton which was the subject of a news article on the front page of *The Hamilton Republican* of November 14th.

The Board of Trustees of the Village of Hamilton, through Mayor William A. Reid, made application to the Works Progress Administration for a grant to build a municipal golf course. The idea found its inception in the willingness of Colgate University to deed to the Village of Hamilton over 100 acres of land east of Hamilton Street and University Avenue for this purpose.

The transfer of the property by deed from the University to the Village was necessary in order to conform to certain requirements in the application form.

All the details of this transfer are known to the various officials and personnel of W.P.A. and the fact that the Village applied for such grant does not mean that it would have to be accepted if given. Also the Works Progress Administration, before final approval, has the power to recall such a grant.

The fact that announcement has been made through the Associated Press that the application had been approved would indicate that the arrangements entered into were acceptable. Under such a proposal the Federal government allocates a certain sum and the Village funds the balance.

The Village was favored to the extent that the amount which the Village would have to sponsor had been obtained in gifts from outside sources, thus eliminating any expense to the taxpayers of the Village.

Since the original application, the Federal government, prior to final approval of the grant, has asked for a further contribution from the sponsor. Until the assurance of this gift can be given no final announcement can be made.

In view of the fact that the Village Trustees felt that our village would indeed be fortunate to have such generous sponsorship without any cost to the taxpayers, and with the thought in mind that this would mean the purchase of a good deal of material locally and approximately $60,000 worth of labor for this community, they voted to take advantage of the opportunity to co-operate with the Trustees of Colgate University in the undertaking.

The Village Trustees had hoped for an opportunity to have the matter complete and in concrete form some time ago. However, it is not now in that shape and will not be for about a month.

Among the practical considerations which influenced the Village Board in this matter were:

1st. Providing work for our people.
2nd. Not one cent of Village tax money required.
3rd. The project when completed would be of permanent value and at no expense to the Village for maintenance.

Another consideration of vital importance to this community is the cordial good will which has always existed in the relations of Colgate University and the Village of Hamilton which is mutually desirable to foster and perpetuate.

Carl W. Baum

The Hamilton Republican, December 26, 1935

Other W.P.A. Projects Completed in Hamilton

Three other projects were constructed in Hamilton with W.P.A. funding and brought employment to many area workers. The projects were the new State road constructed by Grove Hinman's Madison County Construction Company from Hamilton to the "rocks" on Rt. 12B and continuing north to the Cherry Valley Turnpike (joining today's Rt. 20 near Troop's Scoops Ice Cream Stand), the sewer system for the Village of Hamilton and the Federal Post Office in Hamilton, constructed in 1936. In neighboring Madison, the first addition to the Madison Central School, dedicated in 1939, was also funded in part through W.P.A. monies.

Notes of the author

Parlor Golf Revived

In sharp contrast to stories of the golf tournaments raging fiercely on the Seven Oaks course comes news of a new form of the honorable Scotch game, fraternity golf. Two K.D.R.'s, in search of adventure, dug up a couple of putters and balls from some unsuspecting brother's bag, and set out for the expansive living room, Tuesday night.

With a few ash receivers, chairs, a davenport and Toby (?), as hazards, they rigged up a fine miniature golf course, consisting of several dog-leg holes (no pun intended). As they began to play, more of the fellows wandered in, until a large percentage of the house were busily engaged in pawing "pills" from underneath furniture. Now, every night finds all the lights in the front room turned on as the boys amuse themselves.

The Hamilton Republican, October 17, 1935

The Robert Trent Jones golf course design from 1935. This was the second design plan that he had created for Colgate, the first being in 1934. Map photo courtesy of Joseph S. Hope.

GOLF COURSE PROJECT RECALLED

The golf course project has been recalled by the W.P.A. William Reid felt that the chief reason was communication printed in the local newspaper in opposition by a citizen of the village, who happens to be a member of the Colgate faculty.

The stated reason by the Works Progress Administration was that the Village of Hamilton was receiving a great amount of help in the building of the new State highway, the Federal Post Office and a sewer line project.

From Colgate Athletic Council Meeting, January 10, 1936

ADDITIONAL PROPERTY ACQUIRED

William Reid has informed the Athletic Council and the Board of Trustees that two additional pieces of property have been obtained for the golf course project and await approval from the Council and the Trustees. He also recommended that $2,500 be spent for a set of plans from the firm of Thompson and Jones, golf architects.

Mr. Reid also stated that with the additional land, the University could use labor at hand on the current Seven Oaks course and some University labor and build 4 or 5 holes per year.

[*Robert Trent Jones had originally designed a course for Colgate in 1934. This design was to be constructed on the former Dunn Farm and did not include areas to the north of Payne Street. With additional property being obtained it was necessary to have Jones re-design the plans to fit the anticipated new acreage. This is the 1935 plan which is now framed and hanging on the wall in J.S. Hope's office in the Administration building on campus. The properties obtained would be the Wheeler and Hartshorn properties. The Wheeler property is currently portions of holes #13, 15, 16, and 18. The Hartshorn property is now the left side of the dog-leg area of #13.*]

From Colgate Athletic Council Meeting, January 10, 1936

Plans for a Course Continue

The Athletic Council, at its meeting this morning, approved the graded construction of a golf course, condition upon the approval of certain recommendations to the Board of Trustees.

The Athletic Council approved the purchase of two additional properties to complete the land needed for the golf course, provided the Board of Trustees would pay one-half the cost of the purchase, title to the land when purchased to be vested in the University.

The purchase price of this land will not exceed $7,000. The Athletic Council has already approved the expenditure of not more than $3,500, and the Council requests that the Board participate to the same extent.

The Council also stated that they have voted to purchase plans from the golf architects, subject to satisfactory arrangements regarding price and the bringing of plans up to date.

[*The 1934 design from Jones was brought up to date. A hole-by-hole booklet dated September 1936 is in the archives at the Colgate Library. This would be the fourth course that Jones designed in the U.S., following Midvale Golf and Country Club (Penfield, N.Y.), Durand-Eastman Park Golf Course (Rochester, N.Y.), and Green Lakes State Park Golf Course (Fayetteville, N.Y.).*]

From Colgate University Board of Trustees Meeting, January 10, 1936

Payment for Dr. Wheeler's Land

On April 30, 1936, payment was made to Dr. I.N. Wheeler for land purchased for the new golf course. The area was to become holes number 13, 14, and 15 on the new 1935 course plan design.

From Colgate Athletic Council Meeting, April 30, 1936

The Green Lakes Connection

Robert Trent Jones designed the Green Lakes State Park Golf Course in 1935. Using a force of Civilian Conservation Corps workers, the course opened for play on May 28, 1936. The State had no money to pay Jones due to the Great Depression continuing to grip the nation. The agreement was that the State would lease the course to Jones for $1.00 per year for 10 years.

At the end of the contract, under which Jones could keep all of the concession money, he sold the course back to the State. It is interesting to note that Gene Sarazen was at the opening of the course, and in 1939, Robert Trent Jones gave Bill Reid a membership to Green Lakes.

According to an article in the August 15, 1940, edition of the *Syracuse Herald-Journal,* Robert Trent Jones was holding a golf event which featured a hole-in-one contest. The entertainment portion of that contest was provided by none other than Emmett Kelly, the foremost clown prince of his day.

Notes of the author

SQUIRES BEAT CAPTAINS

The Squires defeated the Captains, 3–0, in the first intra-club golf match at the Seven Oaks Club last Saturday, William L. Burke being leader of the winners and William A. Reid captain of the losers.

Scoring for the teams of 15 men apiece was based on one point for total matches, one for aggregate score and one for order of finish.

[*The name "Squire" refers to a local dignitary or lawyer in a small town or rural district. William Burke, Sr., was a lawyer in Hamilton and at one time was also District Attorney for Madison County.*]

The Hamilton Republican, June 25, 1936

PRELIMINARY WORK BEGINS

Preliminary work has begun on the new golf course at Hamilton and the 18-hole layout will be a Colgate University project, according to William A. Reid, Director of Athletics at the school. Robert Trent Jones, who designed and built the new links at Green Lakes State Park, outside of Syracuse, has surveyed the land and marked the projected tees, fairway directions, and greens.

Plans are being drawn up for construction but in all probability actual work won't begin until next spring. It is expected the course will be 6,200 yards off the front of the tees and 6,700 yards off the back. Jones has ambitious plans for making it one of the finest links in this section. Gene Sarazen, noted pro, will probably consult with Jones on the later stages of the work.

[*Sarazen had also consulted with Jones on the Durand-Eastman Park Golf Course in 1934. In 1955, Sarazen consulted with Jones on the Wiltwyck Country Club project in Kingston, N.Y. Also, please keep in mind that the course "on the hill" was called Seven Oaks at this time.*]

Utica Daily Press, September 2, 1936

SARAZEN TO EXHIBIT GOLF SKILL

Gene Sarazen, one of America's greatest golfers, will exhibit his skill with the clubs at 3 o'clock Friday afternoon on the first tee of the Seven Oaks Golf Course. Later at 7:30 o'clock that night he will show golf movies and lecture about the game in the Little Theatre of Lawrence Hall.

Although Sarazen may limit his golfing activity to some driving, chipping and putting around the first tee and the ninth green, there is a good chance that the colorful champion may be persuaded to play a round of golf in a foursome of local or Colgate University players.

Sarazen is being brought to Hamilton mainly through the efforts of William A. Reid, Colgate's Director of Athletics, in order to inaugurate what should be an eventful season in local golfdom. There will be no admission charge for Sarazen's movies.

The Hamilton Republican, May 6, 1937

Gene Sarazen giving an exhibition of his golfing skills before Colgate students in 1937. Courtesy of the Tom Parnell Collection.

THE SARAZEN GOLF EXHIBITION

The golf season at the Seven Oaks Club was launched last Friday with an exhibition by Gene Sarazen, internationally known professional, who shot a 74 for the par 70 eighteen holes despite the fact he three-putted seven greens. A crowd of 1,000 Colgate University students, faculty and townspeople followed the shotmaker around the course and later watched him demonstrate the use of each club in his bag.

James Dalgety, Seven Oaks pro, and several Hamilton enthusiasts took full advantage of Sarazen's appearance to brush up on the theory of their own game. William A. Reid and William L. Burke, respective team captains at the club for the coming year, were two who secured some pointers on the game from the famous pro.

On the first nine Sarazen played with members of the Colgate varsity team—Captain Wes Van Benschoten, Tommy Fay and Burr Horn. He played their best ball and was four down at the turn. On the second nine he was in a foursome with Billy Wells and Jack Morrell, freshman stars, and Ross Adamsen of the varsity. Colgate was finally declared the winner, 5 and 4.

Later that night a large crowd gathered in Lawrence Hall to see motion pictures and hear Gene lecture on golf. During the day Gene also talked with Andy Kerr, and after watching the Colgate football coach's swing, he declared it was sound.

The Hamilton Republican, May 13, 1937

HE TOOK THE NAME OF "SQUIRE"

When Gene Sarazen came to Hamilton for the golf exhibition, it was a homecoming of sorts, for he had visited Hamilton a number of times before. He was good friends with Bill Reid and was soon friends with William Burke, Sr., as well.

Mr. Burke was known as "Squire," that term being used for a country lawyer. Mr. Sarazen admired the nickname so much that he was soon using it for his own. The story comes down to us that he "borrowed" it from a Hamilton lawyer.

[*Information also comes down through the Burke family that it was William Burke, Sr., who invented the "reminder grip." That is a bit of trivia worth talking about!*]

Information from Marian (Burke) Blain

Gene Sarazen hitting from the rough on the 4th hole on the "hill course" and giving a putting demonstration at the 1937 Colgate exhibition. Photos courtesy of Special Collections and University Archives, Colgate University Libraries.

29

Work Is Suspended

Even with the arrival of Gene Sarazen and the exhibition which he gave on the "hill" course, work was suspended on the new golf course project. Bill Reid however was determined to have the course built and will renew his efforts again in 1940.

Notes of the author

4th County Roundup Tournament

Hamilton—The fourth annual Madison County Roundup Golf Tournament will be held on the Seven Oaks course of Colgate University here tomorrow and Saturday with teams entered from the Oneida Country Club, the Oneida Ltd. Club of Sherrill and the Seven Oaks Club.

Medal play will begin at 1:30 tomorrow, the winner being judged county champion. On Saturday, play will begin at 9:30 a.m. The three clubs will enter 12 men each, to play 36 holes of golf. When the 36 holes are completed the team champion will be crowned. The team champion will win "The Little Brown Jug" for one year and will also win permanent possession of a specially designed plaque.

A dinner and the awarding of the trophies will be held at the Colgate Inn, Saturday night. The President of the tournament committee is William A. Reid, of Seven Oaks.

The Hamilton Republican, July 21, 1938

Opposite: *Golfing on the old course "on the hill." The course offered panoramic views of the Hamilton area. Photo courtesy of the Special Collections and University Archives, Colgate University Libraries.*

FOUR. THE 1940s AND SEVEN OAKS DURING WORLD WAR II

Plans for a Course Move Forward

William Reid was in touch with Robert Trent Jones again in 1940 and requested that he create a new design for a course at Colgate. Mr. Jones presented a full proposal in the early part of 1941 and planned to visit Hamilton later in the year to go over the layout of the course. The new design would keep the nine holes "on the hill" and add a new nine on "the flats."

Notes from the files of Robert Trent Jones at Cornell University

Bill Burke's Round of 62

The round of the week was shot on Tuesday by Bill Burke, Jr., who whirled around the course twice with an expenditure of only 65 strokes. Outward bound, he toured the nine holes in a one under par 33; coming home he shaved the norm by two strokes, carding a 32. He was playing with "Ros" Rosengren, Colgate '24.

That ties the record which Jim Dalgety set in 1931 and equaled again last year. Incidentally, Jim holds the nine-hole record—an even 30 strokes.

The Hamilton Republican, July 18, 1940

Trophies to Be Won

In addition to the trophies presented for winning the men's and women's club championships, by 1940 there were also trophies presented for the men's and women's handicap tournaments. The men's award was the William A. Reid Men's Handicap Trophy and the women's award was the Dr. I.N. Wheeler Women's Handicap Trophy.

[*According to an article in the* Mid-York Weekly, *summer of 1951, the Reid Tournament had been reactivated. It had been stopped just prior to WWII. Another article in the summer of 1951 noted that play had been held for the George Cobb Memorial Trophy. This was an Inter-Class Tournament which encouraged participation from all Colgate classes, past and present. We can assume that it had replaced the earlier College Interfraternity Cup. George Cobb was President of the Alumni Corporation and had donated the Dart Farm for the remodeling efforts on "the hill course."*]

Notes of the author

Fire Destroys Caddie House at Colgate

Hamilton—The fifth in a series of fires in this area within the last five days caused an estimated $3,500 loss on the Seven Oaks Golf Course at Colgate University yesterday. Flames destroyed the caddy house with its golf clubs and other equipment.

There was no indication of how the fire started. A coal fire was burning in a stove used for heating water for the showers, but the stove was banked for the night when Jimmy Dalgety, Professional, and Bruce Baker, his assistant, left late Tuesday afternoon. The fire was discovered by a night watchman walking between buildings on College Hill.

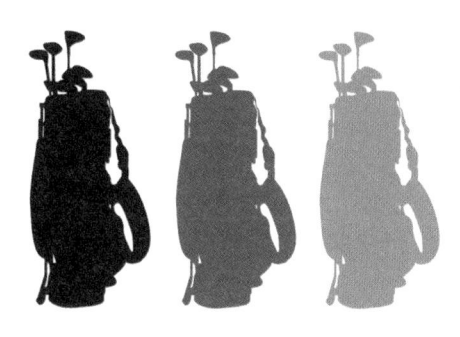

He called the fire department and even though they arrived in a matter of minutes, the wooden structure was already a mass of flames and breaking through the back part of the structure. There was nothing they could do.

Hundreds of students, aroused from sleep in the dormitories nearby, watched the building burn. Some of them lost golf clubs, which had been stored there. William A. Reid, Director of Athletics, said approximately 20 sets of clubs were lost.

Workmen started clearing away the wreckage as soon as it cooled during the day and by night, men working under Harold Dahn, Supervisor of Equipment and Fields, had leveled the ruins.

By night, Reid had engaged an architect. A new caddy house will be built at once, Reid said, and he hopes to make it more modern and better than the one destroyed. The caddy house was built in 1928 near what now is the fourth tee. Later it was moved to its present site, not far from the present first tee and behind Stillman and Andrews halls. Since it has been on its present site it has been remodeled and additions have been built.

The Hamilton Republican, May 22, 1941

SEVEN OAKS WILL REBUILD

Hamilton—Plans for the new Clubhouse on the Seven Oaks Golf Course, to replace the club and caddy house that burned 10 days ago, were announced after a meeting of club members at the Colgate Inn.

According to information given by John W.S. Littlefield, Treasurer of the University, and William A. Reid, the new Clubhouse will be constructed with a large lounge in the center, with locker rooms for men and women on each side, a porch on two sides of the building, a pro shop and a special room to be used for preparing food during club matches.

At the south end of the lounge a fireplace will be constructed and a heating plant will be in the basement. A special room for caddies will be underneath the main structure.

The new building, to cost at least $3,000, will be constructed of wood and stone. It is expected construction will begin next week.

The Hamilton Republican, June 5, 1941

NAMING A HOLE ON THE NEW COURSE

A letter from John W.S. Littlefield to N.F.S. Russell
June 10, 1941

I am giving $3,000 for a hole to be named on the new course for Dr. Melbourne S. Read and called the "Pioneer." The boulder carrying the brass tablet at Hole #1 will be moved to Hole #1 on the new course.

TOURNAMENTS FOR 1941

Events Committee Chairman "Eppie" Barnes, with associates Fred Swan and Jim Dalgety, has announced the remainder of the golf events at Seven Oaks. Included in the schedule will be the "Blitz" Tournament, Mixed Two Ball Foursomes, The Kicker's Tournament, The Sweepstakes Tournament and The Graveyard Tournament.

[*To give you an idea of what these events were, in the Kicker's Tournament, one shot on each hole could be replayed except for putts and in the Graveyard Tournament, each player was assigned a number of strokes and the player that went around the course the farthest was the winner. It was also the final tournament of the year. Everett Barnes' full name was Everett Duane Barnes.*]

The Hamilton Republican, June 26, 1941

An early photo of Everett D. Barnes. Known as "Eppy" to many, he will become the Athletic Director at Colgate in 1955 and will guide the completion of the current Seven Oaks Golf Course. Photo courtesy of the Special Collections and University Archives, Colgate University Libraries.

Golfer Brandishes Mashie

Hamilton—A snorting bull, 11 cows and a horse ambled out on the Seven Oaks Golf Course Monday and Herman Reynolds, of Madison, was given a chance to display his courage and daring as a bull fighter.

Reynolds, having shot a 78 the day before—his best round in the 10 years he has been playing—was having trouble with many of his shots when the animals appeared.

The women golfers fled to shelter when the bull snorted and pawed the ground and some of the male golfers were also easing themselves off the course.

At that point Reynolds missed a shot. Disgusted with his game, he found it a relief to be challenged by a bull. He swung a mashie aloft and chased the bull into the woods. The cows and a horse moved on and there was no interruption after that.

Utica Daily Press, July 23, 1941

Memo from Mr. Russell

Letter from N.F.S. Russell to William Reid
September 3, 1941

Robert Trent Jones was in my office this afternoon going over the layout of the golf course and he expects to see you next week. I told him monies were being collected. Jones thought if in October, we could plow certain portions of the land covering nine holes that we are estimating building, it would help greatly and then next year we could commence to grade and seed them down.

Golfers Dedicate New Clubhouse

Playing the last of their tournaments on Labor Day afternoon, the members of the Seven Oaks Golf Club crowned the season's activities by sitting down in the evening to a picnic supper in the lounge to dedicate the new Clubhouse. Through the efforts of John Littlefield, masons and other mechanics, who worked all day on Saturday, the building was serviceable for this special occasion.

Called upon to dedicate the new building, William L. Burke, Sr., the club's first "Squire," gave a brief and effective sketch of the development of Hamilton's interest in golf from the days when Dr. Melbourne Read and Fred Jones supervised laying out the first course more than twenty years ago. He paid tribute to Dr. I.N. Wheeler, long a member of the Green Committee, who had "given time and resources to improve the course" and William A. Reid, whose influence as head of Colgate's athletic department has been generously used to enlarge and support the entire program.

Following his talk Mr. Burke touched a match to the logs in the attractive stone fireplace, adding that he hoped many happy years were in store for the community's golfing fraternity.

[*William Burke, Sr., died in 1942. He had been instrumental in securing more property for the new course. His efforts to purchase property would be carried on by William Reid and Everett Barnes.*]

The Hamilton Republican, September 4, 1941

The new Clubhouse on the hill course. It replaced the one that burned in May 1941. Beautifully constructed, it became the lodge at the ski hill area when it was moved in July 1965 and is currently the main building for the outdoor education program at Colgate. Photo courtesy of the Special Collections and University Archives, Colgate University Libraries.

THE PLANS ARE TUCKED AWAY

The story has been told for years that the plans for the new course at Colgate were "tucked in the drawer, pulled out twenty years later and the course was then built using the original plans of Robert Trent Jones." The plans were indeed put away, but the reason was the attack on Pearl Harbor to start United States involvement in WWII. As soon as the war was concluded and the regular schedule was again established at the University, the plans were once again advanced through the efforts of William Reid and Everett Barnes.

Robert Trent Jones would be called back and the University would purchase additional property, including the Wheeler home, which would become the Seven Oaks Clubhouse of the future.

Notes of the author

SEVEN OAKS COURSE LIMITS RESIDENTS

Local golfing enthusiasts who have been wondering what effect Colgate's accelerated program would have upon their summer playing, received their answer this week in a letter addressed to members of the Seven Oaks Club by William A. Reid, Director of Athletics.

Foreseeing a much greater demand for the use of the course by students here during the summer, local residents will be restricted to play during the mornings, and in the evenings after 5 o'clock.

[*During WWII Colgate University was selected as a campus site for the Navy V-5, V-7, and V-12 programs to train pilots for the war effort. Our military personnel were to have preference on the golf course. Faculty and alumni were also given preferred times.*]

The Hamilton Republican, March 26, 1942

SHORTAGE OF GOLF BALLS

A serious threat to the enjoyment of the game of golf this summer seems to be the possible shortage of golf balls. Jim Dalgety has a stock on hand now, but to make them last, and go around so that no one is shorted more than his neighbor, he'll ration them out, probably one at a time. If you're a regular player, in the play-every-day-that-it-doesn't-rain-class, you'll probably be able to get about three a week.

The Hamilton Republican, May 21, 1942

DALGETY ASKS FOR GOLF EQUIPMENT

James Dalgety, golf supervisor, sent the following appeal to Colgate alumni and friends this week asking for donations of golfing equipment for the use of the Naval Cadets:

"As you know, our golf course is in grand shape and will be available to the Naval Cadets. The big drawback of course will be lack of equipment, ie., golf clubs and bags.

I know there are many alumni and friends of Colgate who have old and discarded clubs, bags, balls and tees lying in attics and cellars and I know they would be delighted to donate these 'old items' to a cause so worthy.

I will personally mend and repair the clubs and bags in my spare time so that the boys may have this recreation."

The Hamilton Republican, February 18, 1943

FEW GOLFERS ANSWER CALL

With most of his experienced golfers gone or leaving soon for active service, Coach Jim Dalgety is seeking new men to fill out the four-man golf team this summer. Only two candidates answered the call yesterday.

Some difficulty has also been experienced by Coach Dalgety in obtaining opponents, as most colleges have discontinued their golf teams. However, matches will probably be played with Cornell, Penn State, some nearby golf clubs and possibly with Syracuse.

The Hamilton Republican, July 15, 1943

OPERATING AT A LOSS

William Reid reports that the golf course is operating at a loss due to very little play on the course. The general feeling is that we should keep the course open for play for the duration of the war.

[*Not as many military personnel played golf as expected and a large group of townspeople were engaged in fundraising for the war effort and other civic activities. Following the war, the number of players on the course would increase once again.*]

Correspondence from William Reid to the Colgate Athletic Council, September 9, 1943

ANNOUNCEMENT FROM DALGETY

Two announcements were recently made by Jim Dalgety, Seven Oaks Professional. The first is that there will be no golf team schedule for 1944. It is not possible to schedule matches at this time.

The second announcement is that Dalgety is pleading with local golfers to have their golf balls reprocessed as there are no new ones for sale.

[*Golf was added as a varsity sport once again in 1946.*]

The Hamilton Republican, April 27, 1944

Post-WWII with a Fresh Look

With the end of WWII, the United States entered an era of economic prosperity and a sense that all things were possible. Students returned to their normal academic life and the universities that they attended began to make ambitious plans for the future.

Within that vein of thought, two Colgate faculty members, William A. Reid, Colgate's Athletic Director, and Everett D. Barnes, Colgate's Assistant Athletic Director, took the plans that had been created by Robert Trent Jones in 1935 and gave them a fresh look with the thought of building the course that had been delayed for almost twenty years. These were the same plans that Mr. Reid had attempted to implement in 1936 following the failed W.P.A. proposal.

With plans in hand, Reid and Barnes began to approach the Administration and Board of Trustees of the University with their idea. Success was eventually achieved after new plans were again drawn up by Robert Trent Jones. William Reid died in 1955 before the front nine of the new course opened. Everett Barnes continued the work and also successfully pushed through plans for the building and completion of the back nine.

Mr. Lincoln Stafford, a long-time resident of Hamilton can remember the area for the proposed course having been rented by Henry Beecher to pasture his beef cattle and at a later date rented by the Lamb family to raise beans and corn for market.

Notes of the author

Looking at the Plans— A Novel Approach for 18 Holes

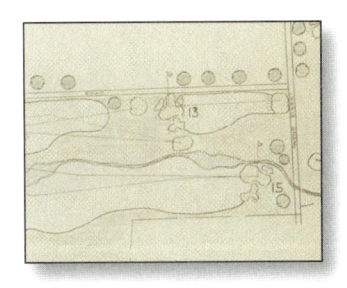

The original 1934 course map and the revised 1935 plan, both designed by Robert Trent Jones, were very different from the course design that we have today. The entrance would have been from Hamilton Street and a Clubhouse was to be built in the area between what is now the 4th tee and the 6th tee. The course would border Spring Street and there were to be only three holes on the north side of Payne Street, instead of our present six.

A campaign was started for an addition to the existing Seven Oaks course. It would have the nine holes "on the hill" and a new nine constructed on the level area. In this novel way Colgate would have an 18-hole course.

From 1935 course map by Robert Trent Jones

Correspondence from Jones to Reid

Letter from Robert Trent Jones to Bill Reid
July 22, 1946

With regard to the approximate cost of building nine holes of the proposed eighteen, I would say that under present conditions it would be between $50,000 and $55,000. This could vary between now and next spring.

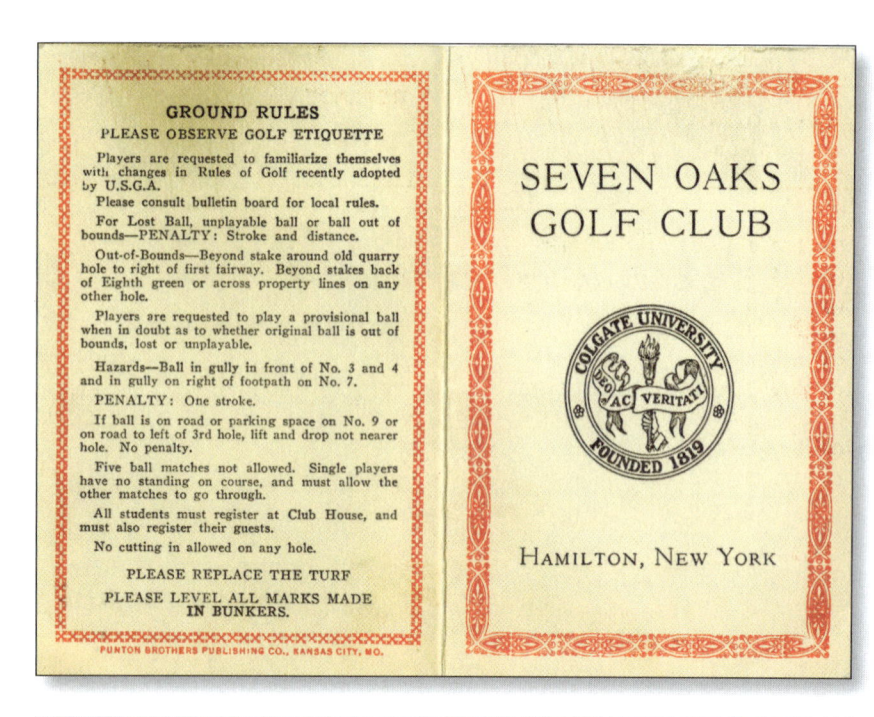

Bill, you are indeed fortunate to have such an ideal piece of golf property, because when completed, it will be as good in its playing quality as the course that I am building for the U.S. Military Academy.

Successful Season

Letter from James Dalgety to Bill Reid
November 15, 1946

1946 was a successful one. The course has never been so busy. Overcrowding has been a constant problem, coupled with the difficult hillside terrain.

I would like to discuss the golf situation and its future with you. 1947 looks to be just as crowded with play.

A later scorecard from the Seven Oaks course "on the hill." Some of the holes had lengths changed since the original design of 1928 and some had been renumbered. This may have been due to campus construction and projects such as the water tower at the top of what became the ski hill area. The scorecard you see here is the one that many Colgate alumni remember as the course that they played when in college. Photo courtesy of the Special Collections and University Archives, Colgate University Libraries.

GOLF FEES FOR 1947

The following are the fees to be charged at the Seven Oaks Golf Club for the 1947 season:
- Resident individual $40.00
- Resident family $50.00
- Faculty (weekly rate) $ 5.00
- Non-residents $ 1.50
- Students $ .25

[*The faculty rate was on a per-week basis because many faculty members took courses or extended vacations elsewhere for a portion of the summer.*]

Colgate Athletic Council Meeting, January 9, 1947

DAHN TO BE COURSE SUPERINTENDENT

With the death of Richard Haley, Sr., Greenkeeper at Seven Oaks, in 1947, the supervision of the course will be under the direction of Mr. Harold Dahn.

[*Mr. Dahn would also be Superintendent of the new course when the front nine was completed through his position in Buildings and Grounds. This appointment began in 1957 during the construction phase of the front nine. He would be appointed as Green Superintendent of Seven Oaks as a full-time position at the Colgate Athletic Council meeting of June 16, 1969.*]

Colgate University Internal Memo, 1948

Bill Reid and Harold Dahn. Mr. Dahn will become the course superintendent on the hill course in 1947 and the new course "on the flats" in 1957. He held that position until 1974. Photo courtesy of the Polly Mahoney Collection.

REID WILL CONTACT JONES

William Reid has been authorized to contact Robert Trent Jones and obtain a survey of costs for development of a course. Mr. Reid said a good deal of the work could be done by the equipment owned by the University and labor could be supplied from the grounds staff.

[*This was still to be a nine-hole course, using the nine holes on the hill to complete the eighteen.*]

Colgate Athletic Council Meeting, January 21, 1949

FIVE — THE 1950s—PLANS FOR A COURSE ARE PUSHED FORWARD

HAPPENINGS AT THE COURSE "ON THE HILL"

Even though plans were again being formulated for a new Colgate golf course, events were still happening on the upper course. The front nine for the new course would not be officially opened until July 4, 1958.

Notes of the author

Golfing on the old course, 1956. The course, located behind the dormitories, offered recreation to the students, alumni, and course members, as well as great views of the area. Photo courtesy of Special Collections and University Archives, Colgate University Libraries.

GOLFERS WILL PLAN FOR SEASON

Members of the Seven Oaks Golf Club will meet in McGregory Hall on the campus of Colgate University next Thursday evening at 8 p.m. for a short business meeting, Jim Dalgety announced today.

The film, "Famous Fairways," will be shown. The schedule for the golf season will be arranged and various committees selected.

Mid-York Weekly, May 15, 1952

Left: *Club Championship winners for the 1953 season—Daisy Roberts and William Burke, Jr. Photo courtesy of the Polly Mahoney Collection.* Right: *An aerial view of the course "on the hill" with a look in the distance at the area that will become the site for the new course. Photo courtesy of Special Collections and University Archives, Colgate University Libraries.*

VICTORY FOR THE WOMEN

As of July 4, 1954, the women of Seven Oaks can wear shorts with a length of one inch above the knee.

Mid-York Weekly, July 1, 1954

"SKINS AND SKIRTS"

The ladies of Seven Oaks have decided to run a "Skins and Skirts" Tournament on July 13. Since the Seven Oaks course lifted their ban on shorts, many of the women have appeared on the golf course with the regulation, one-inch above the knee, walking shorts. Those with the shorts will oppose those with the skirts at the next Ladies' Day event.

Mid-York Weekly, July 15, 1954

A MOVIE AT SEVEN OAKS

A movie will be presented at Seven Oaks Golf Club entitled "Keep 'em in the Fairway." The film will be shown outdoors so bring your chairs. This movie is made possible through the efforts of James Dalgety.

Mid-York Weekly, July 22, 1954

Nine Now—Nine Later

Following the end of WWII, pressure had been building to add nine holes to the golf course due to increased play and the growing popularity of the sport. That movement led to an eight-page publication entitled NINE NOW—NINE LATER. In the detailed explanation, the overcrowding situation was explained, the importance of the course to alumni and friends, the need for good golf facilities to benefit the golf team and the greater percentage of Colgate students who are now playing the game. It could be a great tool for recruiting new students and a focal point for "Town and Gown" relations.

The design was similar to the 1935 plan created by Robert Trent Jones, but with modifications to distances of certain holes and the assumption that additional lands could be purchased along Payne Creek. The arrangement of three holes on the north side of Payne Street was also reconfigured.

The entrance to the course would still be from Hamilton Street and hole #1 was to be where our current #6 is now. The proposal also featured a new Clubhouse, parking area and practice fairway in the area which is today between the 8th tee, the 4th tee and the 5th green. The length of the proposed 18 holes had increased from 6,654 yards to 6,805 yards.

[*It is interesting to note that the entrance to the proposed course from Hamilton Street was originally the road to the Dunn Farm. The house, barns, and milk house buildings all clearly show on the original course designs. The road to the buildings then extended up the hill to Spring Street, across what is now the 3rd fairway. The University had also purchased the Wheeler House from Dr. Wheeler's sister in 1954. Dr. Wheeler was deceased by this time.*]

From "New 18 Hole Golf Course To Be Built at Colgate" brochure, 1954

PERMISSION TO PROCEED

Because of overcrowded conditions, we should proceed as soon as possible with the construction of the proposed new 18-hole golf course. The plan will be to complete as many holes as possible. Authority is given to commence work in late spring of 1955 under the direction of golf architect Robert Trent Jones.

Colgate Athletic Council Meeting, January 21, 1955

RECENT VISIT FROM JONES

Everett Barnes reported that Robert Trent Jones had recently visited Colgate University and re-surveyed the course. His estimate for an 18-hole layout was given and Mr. Barnes asked if the price could be lowered using local labor and equipment.

The work of acquiring additional property was interrupted by the death of William Burke, Sr., in 1942. Mr. Jones suggested the University acquire property rights paralleling University Avenue, as well as some additional property north of Payne Street. These could make the layout of holes better and offer building lots to be sold by the University. The Council selected a committee to finalize plans for the golf course installation.

Opposite: *The NINE NOW—NINE LATER modified course design proposal from Robert Trent Jones. Nine holes were to be built at once and nine holes built at a future time. The entrance to the course was to be from Hamilton Street. Modified course map design proposal courtesy of Special Collections and University Archives, Colgate University Libraries.*

[*According to the Robert Trent Jones files at Cornell University, Colgate had added thirty-five additional acres as of May 14, 1956. Everett Barnes presented the information to the Council because Bill Reid was very ill at the time.*]

Colgate Athletic Council Meeting, September 25, 1955

A later photo of William A. Reid. Bill Reid died in October 1955. Everett Barnes will carry on Reid's work to secure the completion of the new Seven Oaks course. Photo courtesy of Special Collections and University Archives, Colgate University Libraries.

JONES TO PRESENT NEW PLANS

Robert Trent Jones, in a report to the Council, said that he would have the new plans for the course in ten days.

He suggested instead of waiting for good weather in the spring, the Golf Committee should consider and arrange for the clearing of the site before spring to help advance the work.

[*Jones would draw up six sets of plans for the University to consider in building the front nine and the possible construction of an additional nine in the future.*]

Colgate Athletic Council Meeting, January 27, 1956

About Those Sets of Plans

As stated above, Robert Trent Jones designed a number of plans for Colgate University to consider. At this time each of the designs had the entrance to the course from Hamilton Street and varied from nine holes in design to a full eighteen. The final package presented to the University had three nine-hole designs and three eighteen-hole designs. Let's look at some features of each plan:

> **Proposed Plan #1**   9 holes   3,550 yards
> **Proposed Plan #2**   9 holes   3,625 yards
> **Proposed Plan #3**   All 18 holes were to be on the original Dunn Farm. This would have been a very tightly packed design. #1 would have crossed the entrance road from Hamilton Street. Lots are shown which were to be sold on Spring Street. No yardage was indicated for this plan.
> **Proposed Plan #4A and #4B**   18 holes, no yardage indicated. Holes 1–5 and 17–18 were to be on the south side of Payne Street and holes 6–15 were to be north of Payne Street where our present six holes (#s 13–18) are now. Lots for sale were marked out on Spring Street (18 lots) and the upper part of Hamilton Street across from the Sigma Chi fraternity house (4 lots). Plan #4B also had a larger number of holes on the north side of Payne Street than we have now and was a variation of Plan #4A.
> **Proposed Plan #5**   9 holes   3,773 yards
> In this plan, as in Proposed Plan #3, hole #1 crossed the entrance road from Hamilton Street.

From the Robert Trent Jones course design maps at Colgate and Cornell Universities.

Approval from the Trustees

Plans to add nine holes to the Seven Oaks course were approved by the Board of Trustees in New York City on January 27th and work will begin in the spring.

The new nine, designed by prominent golf architect, Robert Trent Jones, working closely with the late William Reid, will be laid out on University owned property skirting the eastern edge of Payne Creek, between University Avenue and Spring Street.

Funds have been accumulating for many years including funding from George W. Cobb '94 and the late F.S. Russell '01. Impetus was given this past fall by a contribution from the American Management Association and a gift from Mrs. Hope Colgate Sloane in memory of her husband, the late William Travers Jerome, Jr. The balance will be sought by quiet solicitation.

Laid out on a comparatively level stretch, the new course will complement the present steep and hilly fairways of the existing nine holes. It will offer the choice of a full 18 holes played consecutively, or, for older persons, an opportunity to play only the level course.

The area to be developed comprises roughly a rectangle of 75 acres bounded on the north by Payne Street, on the west by the private properties on University Avenue, on the east by Spring Street and on the south by Hamilton Street where it adjoins the campus near the present 9th tee.

The committee for solicitation includes Robert C. Roberts and Darwin Lamb for the community and Ernest R. Braun, Jr., '21, William H. Geyer '42, John W.S. Littlefield '22, and Everett D. Barnes '22 for the Alumni.

[*William "Bill" Reid had passed away on October 30, 1955. Everett D. Barnes would continue his work and push the*

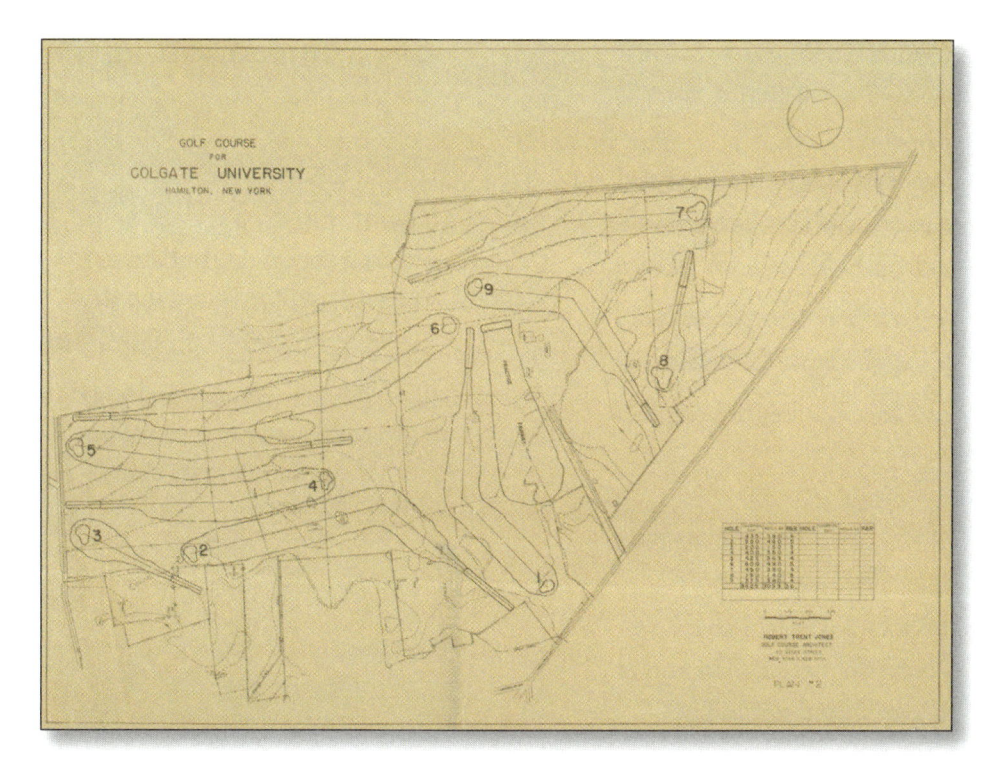

Design Plan #2 featured nine holes to complement the nine holes "on the hill." The design offered 3,625 yards from the championship tees. Map photo courtesy of Colgate University Buildings and Grounds Collection.

completion of the 18-hole course. Mr. Barnes had also been elected as President of the E.C.A.C. in 1955.]

Colgate Maroon, February 8, 1956

Groundbreaking Set for May 12

Groundbreaking ceremonies for the nine-hole addition to the Seven Oaks Golf Course will be held Saturday, May 12th at 2 p.m.

This will enable golfers to play nine holes "on the flat," along with the present scenic course over the upper hills of the valley.

Colgate Maroon, April 11, 1956

Jones Here Again

Robert Trent Jones, the foremost golf course architect, will be in Hamilton again to make further plans on the new nine holes.

Colgate Maroon, May 2, 1956

> **Alternate Plan #1**   9 holes   3,670 yards
> **Alternate Plan #2**   18 holes   7,248 yards
> This plan featured 7 holes on the north side of Payne Street, instead of our present 6 holes.

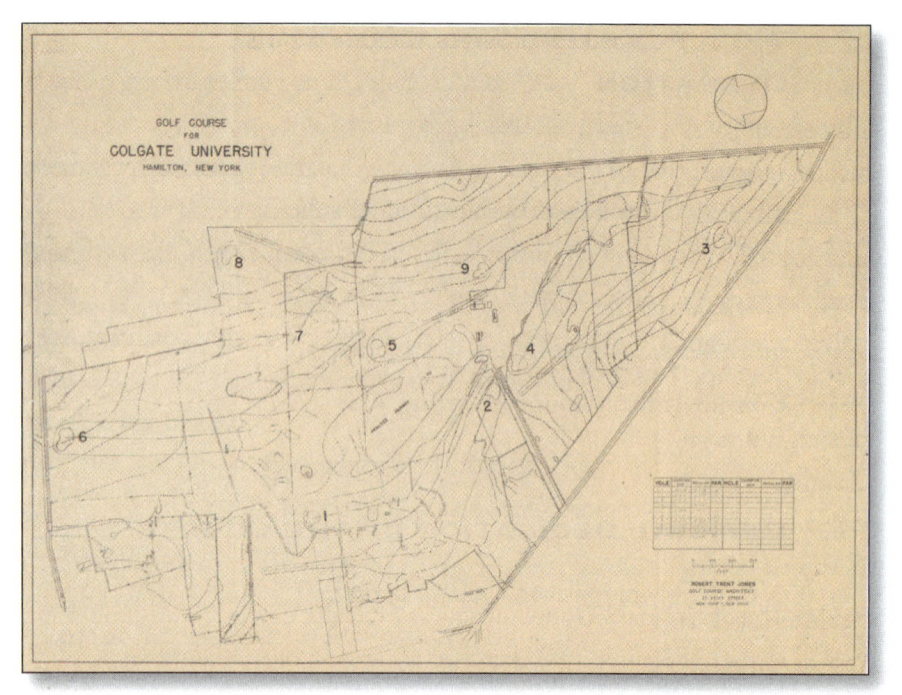

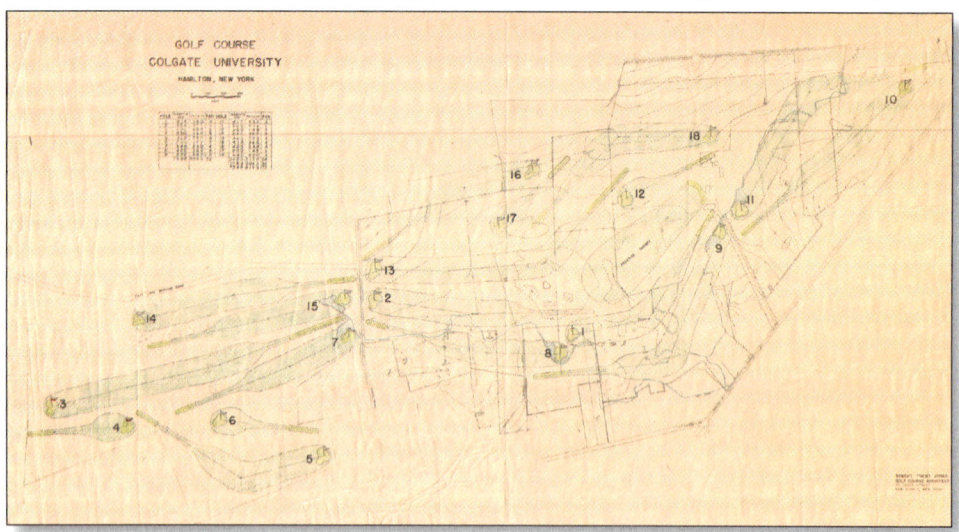

Top: *Alternate Plan #1 featured nine holes and 3,670 yards from the championship tees. It is interested to see the many variations that Robert Trent Jones created while using the same area.* Bottom: *Alternate Plan #2 featured 18 holes, 7,248 yards, and had seven holes on the north side of Payne Street. As yet all of the proposals had the entrance to the course from Hamilton Street. Map photos courtesy of Colgate University Buildings and Grounds Collection.*

BREAKING GROUND SATURDAY

Formal groundbreaking ceremonies for the new nine golf holes will be held Saturday at 2 p.m. Robert Trent Jones is preparing the final plans and equipment will soon be cleaning up the site. The course will run along Hamilton and Payne Streets.

Colgate Maroon, May 9, 1956

CEREMONIES SUCCESSFUL

Groundbreaking ceremonies in connection with Colgate's new nine-hole course "on the level" were conducted Saturday afternoon on Parents Weekend at a spot just across Hamilton Street from the campus. President Case spoke of the history of Seven Oaks.

Ground was broken by Wellington Powell '21, National Chairman of the Colgate University Development Council and a University Trustee. The first ball driven into what is to become the new course was by Jim Davis '58, a member of the current Colgate golf team.

[*The new nine-hole course would be known as the University Golf Course, while the old course "on the hill" would continue to be called the Seven Oaks Golf Club. This would continue until 1963 when the University transferred the name Seven Oaks to the new course with the initiation of the building of the second nine holes.*]

Mid-York Weekly, May 17, 1956

"Pitch and Putt Course"

There was a recurring thought from Everett Barnes and Bill Burke, Jr., through the years that if the plans of Robert Trent Jones were constructed in their current form, the golf course would not be much more than a "pitch and putt" arrangement. The proximity of holes to each other would be very tight and not as enjoyable as they could be if more property were available. As a result, plans from Jones which would feature anticipated property acquisitions became the focal point for the continuation of an 18-hole course.

Information from Marian (Burke) Blain

More Property Is Purchased

During the June 6, 1956, meeting of the Colgate University Board of Trustees, approval was given to purchase the Lamb property (the former Elmer Johnson Farm), the Murphy property and the Myers property, all of which were adjacent to the new golf course. The Board also authorized the division of certain property on the west side of Spring Street, adjoining the new golf course, into lots of not less than 150' frontage, to be offered to the faculty at $1,000 per lot and to other than faculty or staff at $1,500 per lot.

Above: *Groundbreaking for the new nine-hole course on May 12, 1956, included (from left): Robert L. Davis; his son and golf team member, Jim Davis '58; James Leland; James Dalgety; University President Everett Case; Wellington Powell '21; Everett D. Barnes '22; J. Leslie Hart '30; and Robert C. Roberts. The ceremony was conducted on what is now the 6th fairway.*

Left: *A ceremonial first ball was hit from the area along Hamilton Street onto the area of the new 9-hole course by Jim Davis '58, a member of the Colgate golf team. Photos courtesy of Special Collections and University Archives, Colgate University Libraries.*

[The addition of the Lamb property would allow the eventual construction of holes #14 and #17 and portions of #s 16 and 18. Negotiations for the property had been completed by September of 1954 and awaited Board of Trustees approval. The Murphy property completed the lands necessary for the 7th tee and beginning of the 7th fairway and the Myers property would give the room to create the 9th hole in the new plans by Robert Trent Jones. The Myers acreage, which was to be the location for the 9th hole, would later become the driving range area when the 9th hole was moved to its present location.]

Colgate University Board of Trustees Minutes, June 6, 1956

Delayed Plans Now Ready to Go

Plans from Robert Trent Jones are now completed and will be inspected on June 16. Delays had been experienced due to continued changes in the course design.

Jones will stake out the additional nine holes of golf on June 13–14. University forces will perform as much of the work as possible—grading, clearing and cleaning of the site before the contractor appears to install hazards, traps and greens. Mr. Frank Duane will be the site manager representing Mr. Jones.

Seeding is to be done in the spring of 1957 on 75 acres. Completion of the nine holes could be achieved during the late spring of 1957. Weather and maturation of the seeding will determine the actual opening of the nine.

[Work continued during the spring of 1957. Seeding was done, as well as the installation of traps, contouring of greens, and the installation of water lines. By the fall of 1957 it was said that good progress had been made and the course should be ready for play in 1958.]

Colgate Athletic Council Meeting, June 9, 1956

[Mr. Jones had been called back to Colgate to make yet further adjustments to the course layout. His design will result in the front nine that is very familiar to us today. As seen in chapter 6 from a scorecard donated by Dick Eades and the Additional Nine-Hole Plan "B" Design Map featured in the June 4, 1964, edition of the Colgate Alumni News, *we see the front nine as we play it today with the exception of the changes to the original #9 and the new #12. After many design changes over the years, Robert Trent Jones will now have a course design to match the properties that the University had acquired and would acquire in the near future.]*

University Avenue Properties Acquired

A generous gift from Mrs. William Burke, Sr., comprised two of the properties acquired by the University for the construction of the new 10th hole. Other property owners in the vicinity included A. Hengst, W. Smith, Mr. Lowes, C. Roberts, H. Graves, and C. Ault. Although it is not mentioned how many of these properties were acquired, a number were purchased by the University to complete the area necessary for the 10th hole.

Information from Marian (Burke) Blain and contour map (1930s) Colgate University Buildings and Grounds.

Tourney Hole-in-One

Miss Mary Ann Fitzpatrick became the first woman to card a hole-in-one in tournament play at Seven Oaks.

[This was still at the course "on the hill."]

Mid-York Weekly, August 16, 1956

A panoramic view of the construction site for the new golf course in October 1956. A bulldozer is seen at work in the middle of the picture. Photo courtesy of Special Collections and University Archives, Colgate University Libraries.

Rapid Progress

Work on the new nine progressed rapidly over the summer. Grading is done and the water pipes have been installed. Serious play will not begin until the summer of 1958.

Colgate Maroon, September 19, 1956

Bingle, Bangle, Bungle Tournament

In this tournament format a point is given for the first ball on the green, another for the ball nearest the cup and a third point for the first ball in the cup. The player with the most points wins.

Mid-York Weekly, July 11, 1957

Humor on the Links

- A golfer's diet: "Live on greens as much as possible."

- "He who has the fastest cart never has a bad lie."

- When asking his pro how he could hit it further: "Hit the ball as you normally do and quickly run backwards."

- "Its good sportsmanship not to pick up lost balls while they are still rolling." —Mark Twain

- "I have a tip that can take 5 strokes off anyone's game. It's called an eraser." —Arnold Palmer

- "If I hit it right, it's a slice. If I hit left, it's a hook. If I hit it straight, it's a miracle."

Courtesy of the Jim Ford Collection.

49

Tournament Reactivated

The Madison County Roundup Tournament, which had been discontinued during WWII, was reactivated with the Seven Oaks Club, Oneida Golf Club, Kenwood Golf Club and Cazenovia Golf Club represented.

Mid-York Weekly, August 8, 1957

Report on the New Course

In a report to the Colgate Athletic Council, it was stated that fees for the services of Robert Trent Jones were now to be addressed. The Baldwin Construction Company continues to oversee the construction of the new front nine and that students from the college have provided labor during the fall of 1957 and will also help during the spring of 1958. They are involved in picking of stone, raking, and the general clean-up of debris.

It was also reported that the new nine holes will hopefully be ready for play in late spring of 1958.

[*As a point of information, an architect's fee for the design of a course at this time was 10% of the cost of new course construction.*]

Report to the Colgate Athletic Council, October 11, 1957

Reid's Foresight

To emphasize the foresight that went into the planning of the new Seven Oaks Golf Course, Colgate University played Duke in football in 1937 on Whitnall Field.

Bill Reid had wooden ramps made in advance to lead people to the ticket booths. He stated, "I'll have use for these after they've served their present purpose. See that they are stored away carefully," he told his head groundskeeper. Those same ramps are now foot bridges which span the creek that meanders the new golf course.

Shortly after the American Management Association moved in and got itself firmly settled, a golf course, as a necessary recreational facility, became a number one objective. "Our students," as Mr. Appley explained it, "were not conditioned to a mountainside layout which was easily negotiated only by goats and sturdy youngsters. We needed something a good deal less strenuous and are quite prepared to do our share in securing one."

Mid-York Weekly, January 10, 1958

Clubhouse Discussions

Concern has been raised about a proper housing facility for Clubhouse use and direction of golf course traffic. The main topic of discussion in regard to a Clubhouse is the possible use of the Wheeler House and the problems of its rehabilitation. Perhaps the American Management Association could help.

In case this does not work out, consideration should be given to moving two "Vetville" units to the golf course site for temporary use.

[*The University had purchased the Wheeler House in 1954. "Vetville" was the term for the temporary housing units provided for returning military personnel and their families following WWII. The "Vetville" units were located on College Street. They were eventually torn down and the present student housing complex was constructed.]*

Colgate Athletic Council Meeting, January 17, 1958

Lot Size Reduced

The January 17, 1958, meeting of the Colgate University Board of Trustees authorized the size of the lots being sold on Spring Street to be reduced from 150' frontage to 125' frontage and 125' deep. This would allow the sale of ten lots in this area and would help defray the cost of the new golf course.

[*New homes were already being built on these choice lots in 1959.*]

Colgate University Board of Trustees Meeting, January 17, 1958

Renovating the Wheeler House

The Wheeler house is currently undergoing a face-lifting and renovation to ready it for use as a Clubhouse when the University Golf Course opens.

The committee in charge of the program includes Everett D. Barnes, James M. Dalgety and John W.S. Littlefield from the University, Dr. Vernon Gibson, Dr. Montfort Haslam and Robert C. Roberts from the community and Joseph Huther from the American Management Association.

Records indicate the Wheeler house was built sometime about 1835 by Deacon Charles C. Payne, the ninth of sixteen sons of Judge Elisha Payne, who was the founder of the Village of Hamilton and one of the founding fathers of the University.

For many years Payne and his wife encouraged their friends from the community and the students and faculty members from "the hill" to gather in the house. In 1905, the house was conveyed to Dr. Isaiah N. Wheeler, a retired dentist, and his wife. It was acquired by the University in 1954 from Dr. Wheeler's sister.

[*Dr. Wheeler named his home "Belvoir," meaning "beautiful view." Looking out from the Clubhouse today, it certainly does have beautiful views of the Colgate campus and a number of the holes on the golf course.*]

Mid-York Weekly, May 15, 1958

Students Hired for the Project

During the fall of 1957 and the spring of 1958 students from Colgate were hired to work on the golf course project. Raking stones, smoothing rough areas in the new fairways, and collecting debris were their jobs. The work was done by the students before morning classes and it offered the students an opportunity to make some extra income. Their effort allowed the front nine of the course to officially open in the summer of 1958.

The students worked under the direction of Mr. Frank Duane and Mr. John Bauer, the onsite representatives of Robert Trent Jones. Mr. Ozzie Jones was hired to be the day-to-day Manager of the project.

A dump truck unloads sand in one of the new bunkers for the front nine and workers spread sand in the trap in 1958 in preparation for the formal opening to be held on July 4th. Photos courtesy of the Mid-York Weekly *Collection.*

The construction company responsible for the shaping of traps and greens was the William Baldwin Golf Construction Company of Bloomfield, New Jersey.

Information from Arthur Rashap '58 and the files of Robert Trent Jones at Cornell University.

THE FAIRWAY SEEDING MIXTURE

Seeding of the fairways was a huge job. The grass mixture was obtained from Scott's Lawn Care Products of Marysville, Ohio. In all, 500 pounds of seed were used for each of the approximately 75 acres of the front nine. The mixture consisted of 30% Colonial Bent Grass, 30% Kentucky Blue Grass, 20% Fescue, and 20% Domestic Rye. The greens had peat moss in the mixture.

Files of Robert Trent Jones at Cornell University

CRASH PROGRAM SPEEDS COMPLETION

Despite the inclement weather and frequent cloudbursts of recent days, a crash program to ready the new University Golf Course for its formal opening in early July is making steady progress.

Rehabilitation of the Wheeler house into a Clubhouse is also going forward to give Colgate University and the Hamilton community a complete golf facility.

The new nine-hole course supplements the existing Seven Oaks course which also covers nine holes. Future plans call for an additional nine holes for the University course. Seven Oaks (the old course) will be retained once these plans are realized and will be maintained in top condition for the University's physical education program, intramurals and for those golfers who prefer its rugged natural challenge.

The new nine-hole course has been built at a cost of approximately $100,000 and spans 3,620 yards. The completed second nine will extend this to 7,260 yards. The extensive size of its greens and tees will allow play on so-called red, white, and blue courses. One of these courses will be a ladies' nine while the others will be used for the front and back nines with varying pars for the men.

The Wheeler house will offer locker facilities for men and women, modest dining accommodations and a pro shop which will be under the direction of James Dalgety, Colgate's golf coach and pro at the Seven Oaks course.

The 19th century landmark is being renovated through a cooperative program embracing the University, the Hamilton community and the American Management Association. Plans are now being drawn for opening day ceremonies and are expected to be announced in the immediate future.

[*It is interesting to note that in addition to the construction of the front nine, Colgate was also in the process of or just finishing the construction of Chapel House, the new Library, and the Reid Athletic Center. These were busy years indeed for Colgate.*]

Mid-York Weekly, June 5, 1958

Ceremony Plans Are Finalized

A foursome of golfers representing the groups which cooperated in the construction of the new University Golf Course will formally open the course in special ceremonies on July 4th.

Joining in the ceremonies at 1 p.m. Friday the 4th will be Miss Prudence Hawkins, whose father was one of the founders of Hamilton's original golf course. A foursome of Paul Lambert, Squire of the Seven Oaks club, Eugene Adams, Dean of the Colgate faculty, Lawrence Appley of A.M.A. and Jimmy Dalgety, Seven Oaks professional, will open the course for play.

Ground was broken for the new course on May 12, 1956, on the site of the old Dunn Farm. (Transferred to Colgate University by Florence C. Dunn on April 27, 1933.) Once the layout had taken shape under the plans drawn up by noted golf architect, Robert Trent Jones, work was begun on remodeling the 19th century Wheeler home into a Clubhouse.

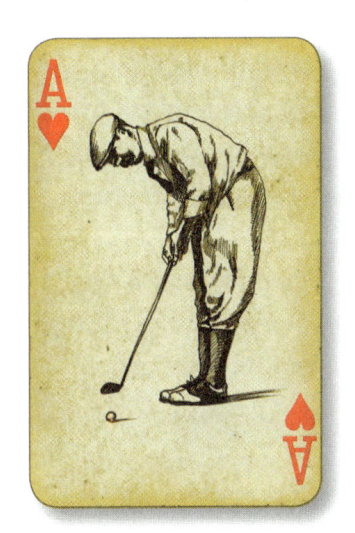

Mid-York Weekly, July 3, 1958

Remembering Those Three Tin Cans

The three tin cans which Dr. Fred Jones and Dr. Melbourne Reed placed on Whitnall Field to serve as Hamilton's first golf course in 1912 became the foundation of a dream which came true at the dedication of the new University Golf Course on July 4th.

Miss Prudence Hawkins, whose father was one of the founders of Hamilton's original golf course "on the hill," cut the ribbon and officially inaugurated the course by hitting out the first ball. The new nine-hole course represents a $150,000 investment and is expected to be the forerunner of an eighteen-hole golf course.

The ceremonies on Friday began with Everett "Eppy" Barnes' tribute to the originators of the new golf course. Joseph Huther, public relations representative for the

American Management Association, was the Master of Ceremonies. He introduced Philo W. Parker, Chairman of the Board of Trustees, and Dean Kallgren, who both gave brief talks.

Joining in the ceremonies were Lawrence Appley, President of the American Management Association, Paul Lambert, "Squire" of Seven Oaks, Betty Baum, President of the women's golf group, Mr. and Mrs. Fred Jones and Mayor James Wardwell of Hamilton, all of whom played a part in the realization of the golf course. Mr. Lambert, Mr. Dalgety, Seven Oaks Club Professional, Mr. Robert C. Roberts, and Mr. Eugene Adams, Dean of the Colgate faculty, also drove out a ball.

In the afternoon a blind bogey tournament was held, with Mr. Dalgety hitting out the first tournament ball. Low scorers in the tournament were Polly Cooley, Pat Shirley, Bill Burke, Paul Lambert and Bob O'Hora.

Mid-York Weekly, July 10, 1958

Above: *Colgate officials, members of the golf course, and townspeople gather for the dedication for the front nine of the new golf course, including a ribbon-cutting by Carl Kallgren, Prudence Hawkins, and Lawrence Appley.*

Right: *Five of the dignitaries at the opening of the front nine posed for a photo after the ceremony. They are from the left: Lawrence Appley, President of the American Management Association; Philo Parker, President of the Colgate Board of Trustees; Carl Kallgren, Dean of Colgate University; Joseph Huther, Director of Public Relations for the A.M.A.; and Everett Barnes, Director of Athletics at Colgate University. Photos courtesy of the Marian Blain Collection.*

Golf Course Committee Established

A golf course committee was established for the University Golf Club on September 19, 1958. According to Everett D. Barnes, the committee will consist of nine members. Five will come from the course membership and four from the University. Duties of the committee will include:
- Regulate conduct of players
- Promote membership
- Develop club activities
- Establish club rules
- Recommend minor Clubhouse improvements

The committee will be subject to the Colgate Athletic Council.

Resolution written by Everett D. Barnes, September 19, 1958

Two Courses, Two Names

Two distinct courses with different names, the University Golf Course and Seven Oaks Golf Course are now available for use. Everett D. Barnes, Director of Athletics, said last week that "It is hoped to use the new course, which is of championship nature in length, for intercollegiate play and championship tournaments."

When the University Golf Course is completed from nine to eighteen holes, it will be 7,200 yards long. The original Seven Oaks course will be reserved for intramural play and physical education instruction.

Colgate Maroon, September 24, 1958

More Land Acquired

Thirty-five acres of new land was purchased for future use in developing the back nine for the new golf course.

[*This was the land mentioned in 1956. Details of the transaction, a closing date, and payment were now complete.*]

Colgate Athletic Council Meeting, October 3, 1958

First Hole-in-One on the New Course

Captain Richard B. Morrin scored the first hole-in-one on the one-year-old University Golf Course. Golf Professional James Dalgety reported that the "ace" was made on the 141 yard #2 with a five iron. Testifying was Kenneth O'Brien, Assistant Professor of History at Colgate University.

Mid-York Weekly, June 11, 1959

Moving the Pro Shop

It is proposed to move the golf pro shop from the Wheeler house to the former Wheeler barn. Plans are to be drawn up to provide a detailed layout. Mr. Dalgety would be in the new facility.

Colgate Golf Course Committee Meeting, January 22, 1959

Green Fees for 1959

The Green Fees for 1959 are as follows:
- Faculty $2.00
- Student $ .50
- Others $2.00*

*On Saturday, Sunday and holidays the fee would be $3.00.

Memo from the University Golf Club and the Seven Oaks Golf Club

---

How About Some Chicken Wire??

To reduce the number of lost balls and to speed up play, it is suggested that chicken wire be placed in the ditches on fairways #1, #4 and the two ditches on #5.

Green Committee Meeting and Report, April 30, 1959

Proposal for a Putting Green

It is recommended that a practice putting green be placed in the area to the south of the Clubhouse porch. A fee could be charged for using it in order to maintain it.

[*The lower putting green was built in 1961. The upper portion was built for the 1977 N.C.A.A. Championship Tournament.*]

Green Committee Meeting, July 1, 1959

Member-Guest Tournament

The first Member-Guest Tournament is occurring at the University Golf Course.

[*This will start a tradition at the new golf course which has continued to this day. It is one of the premier events of the golfing season and one which annually brings many friends together for golf, socialization, and good food.*]

Mid-York Weekly, August 20, 1959

The Cost of Keeping Two Courses

The Colgate Athletic Council has brought up the issue of keeping two courses in operation. More people are playing on the new University Golf Course.

[*By the May 11, 1960, meeting of the Athletic Council, the idea of reducing the old course to three holes was begun.*]

Colgate Athletic Council Meeting, September 25, 1959

SIX. The 1960s and Construction of the Back Nine

We Can't Continue Both Courses

In reports given to the Athletic Council today it was stated that the University can not continue to keep both courses in operation. It is suggested that holes #1, 8, and 9 of the Seven Oaks course be kept.

Buildings and Grounds reported that nine lots on Spring Street have been sold. The money from these sales will just about cover the cost of the additional land purchased for the new golf course.

[*You can imagine the mixed emotions of faculty and alumni over the proposed closing of the "hill course." Part of the old course was also to be used as the site for the construction of a home for the University President.*]

Colgate Athletic Council Meeting, June 10, 1960

"Hill Course" to Close at End of '62 Season

It has been decided to continue operation of the golf course on the hill through the end of the 1962 season and then close it.

[*The course on the hill survived for two more seasons after the initial discussion in 1960.*]

Colgate Athletic Council Meeting, June 8, 1961

A later photo of Jim Dalgety, the first pro at the Seven Oaks Golf Course "on the hill" and the new University Golf Course "on the flats." He retired at the end of the 1962 golfing season and was replaced by Thomas Parnell. Photo courtesy of Special Collections and University Archives, Colgate University Libraries.

"Dalgety Day" Tournament

The James Dalgety Day Tournament will occur on Saturday, May 26th. Twelve area pros, twenty-two former Colgate University golf team members and twenty-four University Golf Course members have signed up to play.

Dalgety is a native of Carnoustie, Angus, Scotland. He served with the 51st Highlanders during WWI and saw action in Belgium, France, and Germany.

[At a testimonial dinner in his honor that evening, Dalgety was presented with a Maroon Citation for his many years of devoted work at Colgate and his instruction in golf to so many of the students.]

Mid-York Weekly, May 24, 1962

A Competition Hole-in-One

Bob Hahnle scored the first hole-in-one in competition at the University Golf Course. The shot was made on the 155-yard 8th hole. Bob used a 6 iron for the shot.

Mid-York Weekly, August 30, 1962

The Length of the First Nine Holes

If we played the first nine holes of the University Golf Course, from July of 1958 until the opening of the back nine in September of 1965, we would have played the following yardages from the championship tees:

Hole	Yards	Par
#1	446	4
#2	141	3
#3	359	4
#4	396	4
#5	498	5
#6	447	4
#7	534	5
#8	189	3
#9	474	4
Total—3,484		**Par—36**

You played the nine holes again for an 18-hole score. The total yardage would have been 6,968 yards and a par 72. After the back nine was completed, the total yardage was 6,915 yards. This was not really a great change and is the yardage that we play today.

Information from a 1961 scorecard courtesy of Dick Eades

Recommendations from the Athletic Council

At the Athletic Council Meeting today, the following recommendations were approved and will be given to the Board of Trustees.

- ✓ The original Seven Oaks course is to be closed at the end of the 1962 season.
- ✓ A committee is to be established to review plans drafted by Robert Trent Jones.
- ✓ The Clubhouse on the original course is to be removed. It will be sold or leased to the Outing Club.
- ✓ The name Seven Oaks is to be transferred to the new course and the stone markers from the original course also transferred.
- ✓ Soil and sod from the original course will be used in the construction of the new back nine holes.
- ✓ Three holes will be retained on the original course for practice purposes.

[Jim Dalgety resigned his position as golf pro at Colgate in January 1963. Creating new ideas to the very end of his career, he established the Annual Junior Golf Tournament in 1962. John Hughes, of Madison, was the first winner of the event.]

Colgate Athletic Council Meeting, October 5, 1962

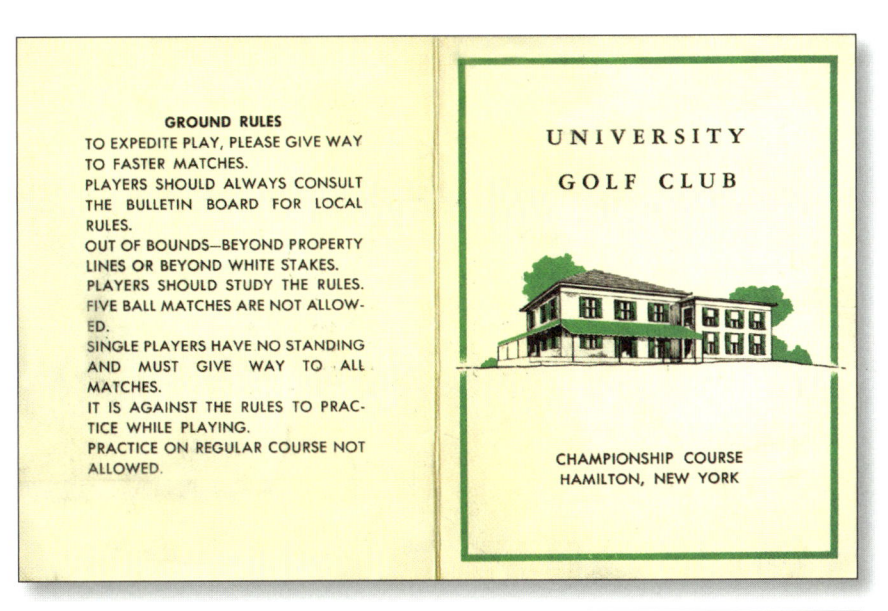

Scorecard for the University Golf Club, 1961. This scorecard was donated to the Colgate Archives by Dick Eades of Earlville. In articles of that time period, the names "University Golf Club" and "University Golf Course" were both used. In March 1963, the name "Seven Oaks" was transferred from the course "on the hill" to replace the University Golf Club (Course) name. Photo courtesy of Special Collections and University Archives, Colgate University Libraries.

The Original Course is Retired

Colgate University, Hamilton, is retiring its Seven Oaks Golf Course on the hill from public play and has transferred the name to the newer University Golf Course. It was revealed that even the Clubhouse at the original course will be moved. The new course uses the former Wheeler House as its Clubhouse. Dr. Wheeler's home was known to many as "Belvoir," meaning "beautiful view."

Construction materials for the back nine of the new course will be obtained, in part, from many of the holes on the old course. Three holes on the original course will be maintained for physical education classes, intramurals, and practice by students.

Officers of the golf course are Rush Carrier, President; George Halloran, Vice-President; Fred Spooner, Secretary-Treasurer.

Utica Observer-Dispatch, March 3, 1963

Appointment of Thomas Parnell

Everett D. Barnes, Athletic Director at Colgate University, has announced that Thomas Parnell, assistant coach in football and golf at Colgate, has been named by the University to the post of Professional at Seven Oaks Golf Course.

This photo was taken soon after the hiring of Thomas Parnell. From the left are pictured Bill Burke, Jr., Paul Lambert, Thomas Parnell, and Rush Carrier. Spring had not yet fully arrived but all four were anxious to play. Photo courtesy of the Mid-York Weekly *Collection.*

Robert Trent Jones had visited Colgate many times in the past to inspect new properties acquired by the University for the golf course expansion and to present new design plans. In this photo, he is third from left. Also pictured are from the left: Thomas Parnell, James Dalgety, and Everett Barnes. Photo courtesy of the Tom Parnell Collection.

Parnell will take over professional duties from Jim Dalgety who has retired after 32 years. Dalgety, Colgate's first professional, will devote his time to teaching golf classes at the University.

Parnell is a graduate of St. Cloud State and coached the Sheboygan, Wisconsin H.S. golf team following graduation from St. Cloud. Parnell, wife Marilyn, and children reside at 19 University Ave. in Hamilton.

The course, formerly known as the University Golf Course, adopted the Seven Oaks course name when Colgate retired the original Seven Oaks course "on the hill."

[*Tom Parnell was hired at Colgate in June of 1960. Parnell and Harold Lahar, Colgate football coach, would co-coach the Colgate Golf Team during the 1963 season.*]

Utica Observer-Dispatch, April 20, 1963

JONES WILL VISIT IN APRIL

Mr. Robert Trent Jones is expected to visit Hamilton on April 23–24 for the purpose of making recommendations in regards to the new nine-hole addition to the Seven Oaks Golf Course.

Golf Advisory Committee Meeting, April 14, 1964

WILLIAM BALDWIN DUE TO ARRIVE

There is a good possibility that the new nine could be started this summer. Mr. Baldwin, golf contractor, is due to arrive tomorrow to inspect the site for the proposed nine holes.

Golf Advisory Committee Meeting, May 25, 1964

JONES GEMS

The life of Robert Trent Jones was filled with many memorable quotes and statements. Some of his most famous issued during his long and illustrious career include:

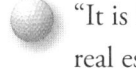

- "It is impossible to lengthen most courses due to real estate restrictions, so it is necessary to take other measures. You can lengthen the rough, grow more trees or add tongue areas to the greens."

- "Every hole should be a hard par but an easy bogey."

- At age 93 Jones awoke in a hospital bed and was told by his sons that he had a stroke. His response was quick and to the point: "Do I have to count it?"

- After working on the Baltusrol Course in New Jersey, the club's committee expressed concern over a par 3 which had been lengthened 70 yards by Jones and ringed with water. Jones borrowed a four-iron, launched a perfect drive toward the hole, which bounced once and fell into the cup. "Gentlemen," he said, turning to the committee members, "the hole is eminently fair."

- "Designs for courses should have bunkering with flashes of sand set off with jagged edges, to emulate the natural look of windblown dunes."

- A Jones course "will feature extremely long tees, fairways pinched on one or both sides, huge greens protected by elaborate bunkers and where possible, a stream or man-made lake to come into play."

Articles from the Robert Trent Jones Society

REPORT ON THE COST OF THE NEW NINE

Mr. J. Leslie Hart has submitted a report to the Buildings and Grounds Committee of the Board of Trustees for the construction of a new nine to the Seven Oaks Golf Course, at an estimated cost of $111,200.

Robert Trent Jones, golf architect, and Baldwin Construction Company are prepared to design and build the course, pending approval.

[*The proposal was approved by the Trustees that same day. The original estimate of costs was $140,000. That figure had been reduced by the offices of Robert Trent Jones and William Baldwin. Colgate would provide labor for the project from their crews and also local labor would be obtained. For example, Louie Lamb was hired to do the finished work on fairways and rake the slopes to tees, bunkers, and greens in preparation for seeding. At the time of the construction of the back nine, Colgate was also building the Dana Arts Center and had received funding for the Olin Science building and the Cutten housing complex.*]

Colgate Athletic Council Meeting, June 5, 1964

Robert Trent Jones had worked with Colgate University since 1934 and had created many course designs for them. His final design has proven to be a challenge to golfers of all ability levels. Photo from the 1977 N.C.A.A. Tournament Program.

Final Revision Ideas

From a letter to Robert Trent Jones from Everett D. Barnes
June 9, 1964

The Board of Trustees of Colgate University at its annual June meeting has approved the proposal to extend the present Seven Oaks Golf Course to eighteen holes based on the revised estimate which was forwarded to you and Bill Baldwin.

The new layout and design you submitted is excellent and I agree with you, will give us an outstanding golf course. When you were in Hamilton we discussed the possibility of reserving enough property at the north end of the property and in the proximity of hole number 17 to provide an area of approximately 200 ft. along the boundary line which would enable us to sell that property in quarter acre plots to provide additional income.

While this would be advisable from our point of view, I do not want to jeopardize the layout. I wish that you would consider this possibility and let me know if it is feasible and should be done from a practical point of view.

[*Mr. Jones responded that from a design perspective it was not a practical idea to change the area of #17.*]

Design Plans Are Finalized

Changes in the plans for the back nine were made as late as July of 1964. The route plan was finalized on 7-20-1964, following the design outlined in the—Additional Nine-Hole Plan "B" rendering on 6-4-1964. That particular plan

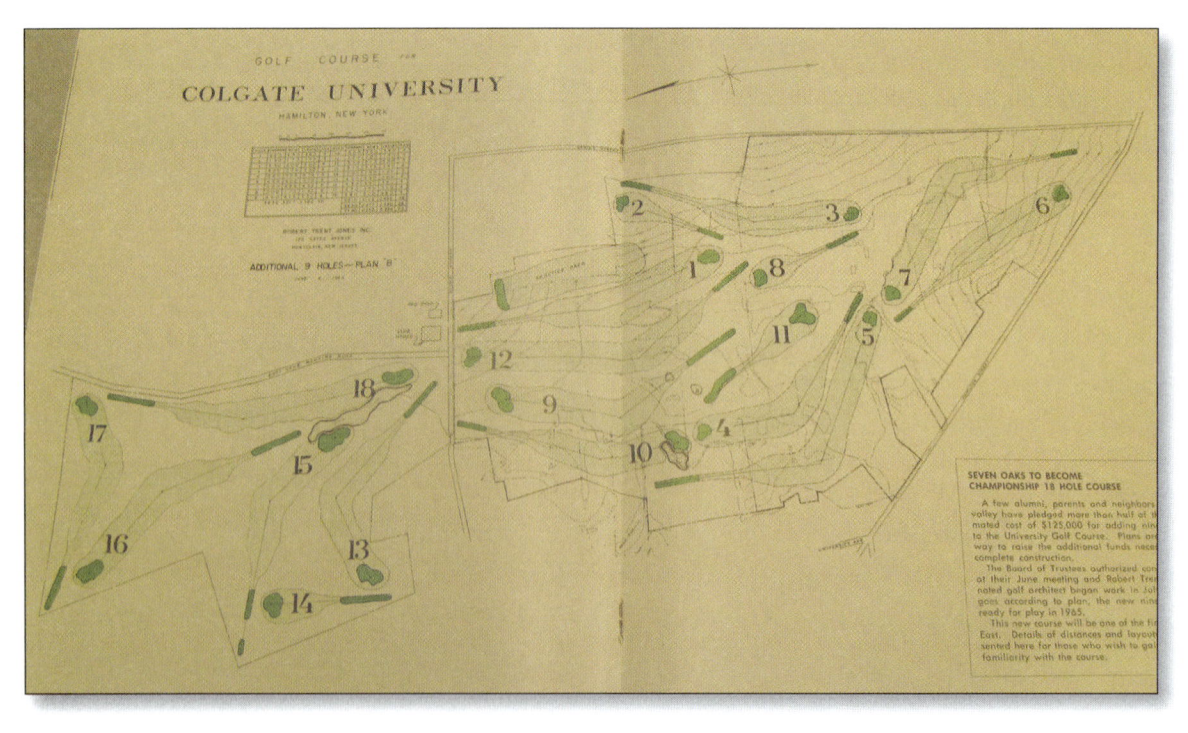

The Additional Nine-Hole Plan "B" Design Map is shown here and is familiar to all who have played at Seven Oaks. It was featured in the June 4, 1964, edition of the Colgate Alumni News. *The hard work of Robert Trent Jones will finally pay off in a "gem" of a course. Photo courtesy of Special Collections and University Archives, Colgate University Libraries.*

had 7,140 yards from the championship tees.

It is interesting to note that a design plan dated as late as May 25, 1964 showed the tee for the 9th hole beginning at the end of the former driving range area and the 9th green being near the road where the former driving range tee box used to be. The driving range in this plan would be in the area where #9 is today. Plans from Robert Trent Jones were still evolving and changes were being made.

By June 4, 1964 the "Additional Nine-Holes Plan "B" was formally adopted. That plan is shown at left and is one which is familiar to all who have played Seven Oaks. Even this plan was modified once more in July of 1964. The yardage from the Championship tees had been increased to 7,170 yards. However, when the final construction work was completed, our present yardage of 6,915 was realized.

[*In discussions with golf course design specialists and club professionals we find out that the yardage will vary from plan to plan due to variables such as the slope of the land, angle of the tee boxes, proximity to roadways, variations in the final size of greens, and the final size of tee boxes. It is not unusual to see these changes and, as such, the site manager for the project will make modifications as needed.*]

Files of Robert Trent Jones at Cornell University

Progress Is Noted

It is reported to the Athletic Council that construction of the new back nine for the course is underway. Extra equipment has been purchased and additional labor has been required to complete the clearing of trees and brush and also to change the course of Payne Creek. Ponds have been dug in front of greens. The cost of the project is now $124,000.

[*Extra labor was supplied by Carl Isbell, Sr., of West Eaton. He performed the additional bulldozing work. Materials from the old course were used in the construction of the tee boxes and greens of the back nine.*]

Colgate Athletic Council Meeting, October 2, 1964

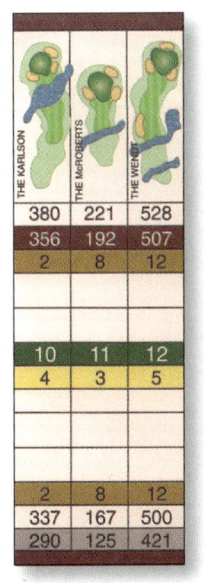

Constructing #s 10, 11, and 12

The purchase and donation of additional property made it possible to redesign the plans for the new back nine. The area for #10 was very wet and swampy and would need a great amount of fill to adequately raise it above the water table. What had been an area for cattle to graze was now to become the 10th and 11th holes and the new 9th hole for the back nine project.

With the decision to move the driving range to the left side of #1 tee and fairway, the plans called for a new 9th hole to be constructed and the former 9th hole to be lengthened to become the new 12th hole.

In constructing the 9th hole, the hill was removed in the area of our present forward tee on #9. You will notice the remains of the hill on the left side of the fairway by the forward tee and on the right side of the fairway with evergreen trees planted on it. The dirt was used to form the 10th fairway and raise it above water level.

The former 9th hole tee box area is now the forward tee for #12 and a new tee box was built for the back tees on #12. This explains the reversal of #9 and #12 that we have heard about for many years.

This aerial photo circa 1977 gives the reader a look at our new course. The evergreens were planted in 1966–67. Photo from the 1977 N.C.A.A. Tournament Program. Photo courtesy of the Richard Carroll Collection.

The new 10th hole featured a dogleg to the left and an approach that had to carry a pond. It is truly a magnificent golf hole. The 11th hole, a long par three, was well-bunkered and the new 12th hole now had adequate length for a par five. And just for a little greater difficulty, the 12th hole featured a fairway bunker on the left side just where an errant tee shot might fall. The three holes were well-conceived and created a flow of play to the remaining six holes across the road.

[*It is only fitting that from 1934 to 1964, we have found 13 different course designs submitted by Robert Trent Jones. Changing events in the world (the Great Depression and WWII) and property acquisitions by the University led to the variations in design. Our beautiful course, as a result of those changes, attests once again to the fact that 13 is indeed a lucky number for Colgate.*]

Plans of Robert Trent Jones and interviews with Marian (Burke) Blain and Lou Lamb

A Brief Biography of Robert Trent Jones

The following is a brief biography of the golf course designer responsible for the championship course that we now enjoy. His association with Colgate University spanned the time of his initial design in the early 1930s, through successive changes in design plans culminating with the opening of the back nine in 1965.

The work of Robert Trent Jones, Sr., always reflected a high degree of expertise and he was able to adapt his designs to fit the changing land acquisitions which Colgate was lucky enough to obtain. His initial design or modifications to more than 400 courses in the United States and around the world attests not only to his golf course architectural skills but also to his devotion to the game of golf.

- Born in Ince, England, in 1906.
- Emigrated with his parents to Rochester, New York, in 1911.
- Was a scratch golfer in his early teens.
- Student at Cornell University.
- Designed his own course of study in golf course architecture while at Cornell.
- Formed a partnership with Canadian golf architect Stanley Thompson in 1930.
- The firm was known as Thompson, Jones & Co., with offices in Toronto and New York City.
- Married Ione Tefft Davis of Montclair, New Jersey, on May 11, 1934.
- His wife was raised in Montclair, New Jersey, and was a graduate of Wells College.

- Raised two sons, Robert Jr. and Rees.
- Left the firm of Thompson, Jones & Co. in 1938 to form his own company.
- That company would later be located in Montclair, New Jersey.
- His lead assistant for more than 30 years was Roger Rulewich.
- Was granted membership to the Royal and Ancient Golf Club of St. Andrews in 1972.
- In 1990 his architectural firm was awarded the construction of a series of 18 courses in Alabama which has become known as the Robert Trent Jones Golf Trail.
- Won every prestigious award given for golf course design.
- Robert Trent Jones died on June 14, 2000. His wife had passed away in 1987.
- By the time of his death, Robert Trent Jones had designed or redesigned more than 400 courses in 45 states and 35 countries.
- His designs have been the setting for 20 U.S. Opens, 12 P.G.A. championships, and 47 other national championship events.
- The Robert Trent Jones Collection at Cornell University, donated by his sons in 2009, contains more than 400 golf course blueprints and 200 boxes of papers and memorabilia from his life's work.

Obituary of Robert Trent Jones, *New York Times*, June 16, 2000; interview with James Hansen, Auburn University; and notes of the author.

The Clubhouse with two enclosed porches and Pro Shop in the early 1960s. James Dalgety ran his Pro Shop business from the barn, as did Thomas Parnell when he was hired. The author worked for Parnell in the converted barn during the summers while going to college. Photo courtesy of the Marian Blain Collection.

Watering System Installed

The Athletic Council has given the approval for the installation of a watering system in conjunction with the back nine holes. It will be installed on the back six holes at this time, with more installation on the other holes to be done at a later date.

[*In the minutes of the Colgate Athletic Council meeting of May 24, 1968, a watering system was approved for the first twelve holes of the golf course to be completed by the fall of 1968. This point was also referenced in an article in the* Utica Daily Press *of July 27, 1969, by Raymond Krehel stating that one of the summer projects at Colgate would be the "installation of drainage and irrigation systems at Seven Oaks." Earlier reference to installing water lines in 1957 had to be modified due to the changes in course design for the back nine.*]

Colgate Athletic Council Meeting, October 2, 1964

An aerial view of the new Seven Oaks Golf Course dated July 16, 1965. The traps on #9 had not been filled with sand at this point. We also notice that the clusters of evergreens along the fairways are missing. They will be planted in 1966 and 1967. The back nine would officially open for play on September 4, 1965. Photo courtesy of Special Collection and University Archives, Colgate University Libraries.

A Pond to Irrigate the Course

At the time of the building of the second nine, a proposal was made to build a large pond and pump house to the right of the 7th fairway, from the second bridge all the way to the area of the green, in order to have a way to irrigate the golf course and save the cost of a water bill to the Village of Hamilton. Since the area selected is very wet, the idea of a pond would have been very feasible.

The idea did not reach fruition because the village protested that the loss of revenue would impact village finances too much. The University abandoned the idea and we continue to be connected to the village water system.

Notes of the author

Caddy House Will Be Moved

The Athletic Council has approved removing the Caddy House from the old course; it will be used by the Outing Club/Hamilton Pistol Club, and will be moved to Trainer Hill.

Construction of the new nine is now completed and waiting for full germination. Llewellyn Lamb, Jr., has been appointed to help Harold Dahn in the supervision of the course.

[*The Clubhouse/Caddy House from the old course was moved to the ski hill in June of 1965. The building was 45-feet square, weighed between 40 and 50 tons, and was brought down the ski hill and placed near the bottom of the ski slope area, on the left side.*]

Colgate Athletic Council Meeting, May 28, 1965

Violation of Conservation Codes

The New York State Conservation Department has found Colgate in violation of Conservation Codes. In order to rectify the situation, the University needs to:
- Install nine small dams along the stream.
- Grade and seed the stream banks.
- Create pools for fish propagation.
- Install additional drainage along the stream.

Hamilton Farm Equipment Company has agreed to do the work as they did much of the original work.

[*Lou Lamb and his sons had previously done the grading and raking of the fairways, bunkers, and tee boxes and the installation of water lines. He performed the work required along Payne Creek. Lou owned Hamilton Farm Equipment Co.*]

Memo to the Colgate Athletic Council from Everett D. Barnes, August 18, 1965

Everett Barnes as he appeared in August 1965. Mr. Barnes had been instrumental in bringing the full eighteen holes at Seven Oaks to fruition. Photo courtesy of Special Collection and University Archives, Colgate University Libraries.

Driving Range to Open

Everett Barnes has reported that the new driving range is also scheduled to open in 1965. The range came about as a result of some changes in the location of the first hole on the new course by Robert Trent Jones and moving the 9th hole to its present location.

[*During the summer of 1965, Junior Golf instruction was also started. Recorded numbers from 1968 show 76 young golfers in this annual event. As a result of this program many fine golfers from the Seven Oaks Golf Course will get their start in recreational golf and the golf industry as a career.*]

Memo to the Colgate Athletic Council, August 18, 1965

Back Nine Ready for Play

The 10th tee will be the site for brief ceremonies at 1:30 Saturday afternoon, September 4, to mark the opening of the new section of the Seven Oaks Golf Course in Hamilton.

The final touches are being applied to the additional nine holes which were laid out last fall and barring inclement weather, the new area will be available for play for the balance of the season. Total yardage for the 18 holes is approximately 6,800 yards, with a par of 72 for men. Chairman for Saturday's opening event is Everett D. Barnes, Athletic Director at Colgate University. University President Vincent M. Barnett, Jr., and James F. Dickinson, Vice-President for Development at Colgate, will speak at that time.

[*The first shot from the new 10th tee was made by Bill Burke as part of the opening ceremonies. In a report to the Athletic Council on September 17, 1965, Everett Barnes stated that the reaction to the new nine was favorable.*]

Mid-York Weekly, September 2, 1965

Materials Used to Make a Green

When we enjoy a round of golf at Seven Oaks and marvel at the condition of the greens, many people have asked about the materials used in the construction of a green.

In interviews with Louie Lamb, who was working on the back nine during the time of its construction, and Jon McConville, our current Course Superintendent, we have a listing of the materials.

The base of the green is a layer of fine crushed stone. Next, a layer of a peat moss-type material is used, followed by a layer of native soil, and finally a layer of sand. The process of aeration and the application of sand, which Jon does on a yearly basis, aids in keeping the green in perfect condition.

Interviews with Lou Lamb and Jon McConville

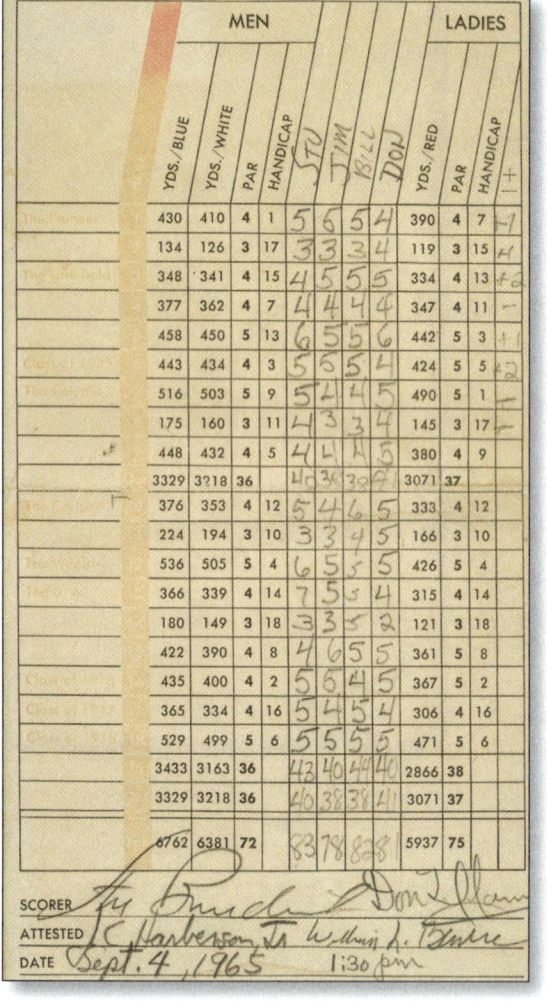

The scorecard for the first foursome off the new back nine at Seven Oaks. Playing in that foursome were Stuart Benedict, Jim Harberson, William Burke, and Don Tiffany. Photo courtesy of the Seven Oaks Clubhouse Collection.

Year-End Golfers

December 30th brought spring-like weather and with it, Hamiltonians Paul Lambert and Bill Burke played what would go down as the last twosome of 1965 on the Seven Oaks Golf Course.

[*Four weeks later our area experienced the blizzard of 1966.*]

Mid-York Weekly, January 6, 1966

HUMOR ON THE LINKS

- "What a shame to waste those great shots on the practice tee."

- "I'm hitting the woods just great, but I'm having a terrible time getting out of them."—Harry Toscano

- "Golf is a game in which you yell 'fore,' shoot six and write down five."
  —Paul Harvey

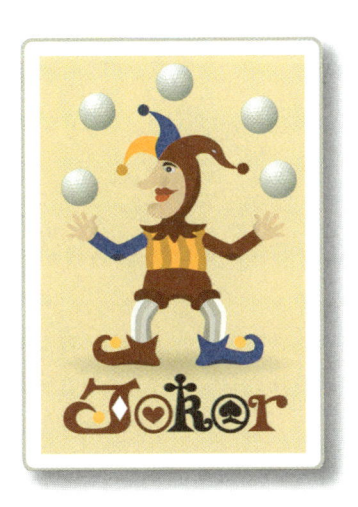

- "Real golfers don't cry when they line up their fourth putt."

- "My golf score seems to improve considerably when I have the scorecard."

- Definition of golf: "A sport in which the ball usually lies poorly, but the player well."

Courtesy of the Jim Ford Collection.

TREE PLANTING AND CLUBHOUSE OPERATION

It is reported to the Athletic Council that a tree planting program is in progress and will be continued. The Clubhouse, which has been operated by the Golf Committee, has been turned over to the Colgate Inn.

[*The arrangement with the Inn was not successful, according to a report in the Athletic Council Meeting of September 16, 1966.*]

Colgate Athletic Council Meeting, May 27, 1966

OFFICIAL DEDICATION OF THE COURSE

The Seven Oaks Golf Course was officially dedicated on June 4th as part of Reunion Weekend activities at Colgate University.

Dedication ceremonies were conducted at the All-Alumni Luncheon in the Reid Athletic Center and focused on the naming of twelve of the eighteen holes which were contributed by individuals and organizations.

Mid-York Weekly, June 9, 1966

NAMING OF THE HOLES AT SEVEN OAKS

1 **THE PIONEER** In honor of Dr. Melbourne S. Read, who had the vision, courage, and faith to pioneer golf at Colgate in 1917. Let's play the game as he would have us—"Always as Gentlemen."
2 **THE BARNES** In honor of Everett "Eppy" Barnes '22 by the Class of 1922.
3 **THE LITTLEFIELD** Donated by classmates and friends of John W.S. Littlefield '22. Mr. Littlefield was Treasurer of Colgate University 1936–1964.

4   **THE ROBERTS**   In honor of Bob and Daisy Roberts. It was a gift from Polly and Chuck Cooley '54.

5   **THE WHITE EAGLE**   Given by the American Management Association, Inc.

6   **CLASS OF 1932**   Dedicated to its members and the spirit that is Colgate, June 1957.

7   **THE COLONEL**   In memory of Colonel Austen Colgate, for many years a Trustee of Colgate University.

8   **THE COTTERELL**   In memory of Wesley M. Cotterell, Class of 1919.

9   **CLASS OF 1935**   Given by Carl J. Kreitler '35.

10 **THE KARLSON**   In honor of Mr. and Mrs. George C. Karlson.

11 **THE MCROBERTS**   Dedicated by the University in honor of Jim and Frances McRoberts '24.

12 **THE WENDT**   In honor of Alvina and Herman Wendt '27.

13 **THE D.A.**   In memory of William Travers Jerome H'28, District Attorney of New York County, 1901–1909; and William Travers Jerome, Jr., Trustee of Colgate University, 1919–1952 and States Attorney of Bennington County, 1943–1951.

14 **THE HAL LAHAR**   Dedicated to Harold "Hal" Lahar by the Maroon Council.

15 **THE PRESIDENT**   Given by the American Management Association, Inc., for the Presidents Association, Inc.

16 **CLASS OF 1916**   Given as a 50th Reunion gift.

17 **CLASS OF 1917**   Presented to Colgate University in honor of the Class of 1917 by Helen and John Dunn.

18 **THE CLASS OF 1918**   Given as a 40th Reunion gift.

Research of the Author

MORE TREES AND MARKETABLE LAND

It is reported that the landscaping program is being carried forward. Both evergreen and deciduous trees are being planted around the course.

The continued report says that there is land adjoining the course that could produce income from a sale as building lots, provided that it is developed.

[*Mr. Irmin Mody, of Sherburne, owned a landscaping company at this time and the trees were planted by his crew. Harold Lahar, Colgate University Athletic Director, had toured the course and helped to decide where clusters of trees, mostly evergreens, were to be planted.*]

Colgate Athletic Council Meeting, January 20, 1967

DISPOSE OF YOUR PRIVATE CARTS

The Seven Oaks Advisory Committee recommended that private golf cart owners would have two years to dispose of their carts at the course. This will give more room in the small cart shed for carts to be rented to members and guests.

[*This was eventually done at the end of the 1968 season.*]

Seven Oaks Advisory Committee, February 15, 1967

FEES FOR THE 1968 SEASON

The following fees have been established for the 1968 season at Seven Oaks:

Season	Resident Family	$200
	Resident Individual	$160
	Junior	$50
Daily Fees	Students	$1.50
	Faculty and Wives	$2.00
	Alumni	$4.00
	Others	$5.50

Memo from the Seven Oaks Advisory Committee, Spring 1968

MCCORMICK PROPERTY PURCHASED

The Athletic Council has authorized the purchase of the Ella McCormick property to be the site of the new maintenance shed. The house on the property is to be rented for now.

The Council has also accepted the idea of naming two holes on the course in honor of Everett D. Barnes and James C. McRoberts.

[*The new maintenance building was constructed by Don Burch of Virdon Estates, Inc. It was built in 1969. The parking lot on the roadside of the building had been the site of the McCormick home. The original maintenance building was located between #8 tee and #4 tee. It had been one of the buildings on the original Dunn Farm property. Two small concrete foundations from the original farm buildings are still visible on your way from the 3rd green to the 4th tee.*]

Colgate Athletic Council Meeting, October 12, 1968

VANDALS HIT GOLF COURSE FOR THIRD TIME

For the third time in less than six months, vandals have raised havoc with the greens at Seven Oaks. In mid-May the 7th green was cut up. On the weekend of May 25–26, the 16th green received similar treatment.

Last Friday night or early Saturday morning, damage was done to the 4th, 5th and 11th greens. Damage was estimated to be over $2,500. Rakes, flag poles, ball washers and tee markers were also destroyed or stolen.

[*In later articles from the* Mid-York Weekly, *it also told of cars doing "wheelies" on the course. One car even got stuck in a sand trap and the two young men abandoned the car. They were arrested later that day.*]

Mid-York Weekly, October 24, 1968

SNOWMOBILES WELCOME!!

Have you looked at the vast expanse of Seven Oaks Golf Course? If you're a snowmobiler you probably have.

Up to now the operators of the golf course have taken a dim view of the snow buggies that have left damage to traps and greens.

This winter, Greenkeeper Harold Dahn is marking each green with flags around the perimeter and says that snowmobiling will be permitted as long as drivers stay clear of the areas so marked and any bare spots on the course. This policy will be in effect as long as the snowmobilers cooperate.

Mid-York Weekly, November 27, 1969

SEVEN — THE 1970s AND 1980s—TOURNAMENTS HIGHLIGHT EVENTS AT THE COURSE

PROPOSAL FOR NEW FACILITIES AT SEVEN OAKS

Harold W. Lahar, Director of Athletics, will propose to the Board of Trustees that the Seven Oaks Golf Course be made a private country club.

The corporation chosen would lease the course from the University and construct a building complex with dining room, meeting room, locker rooms, showers, a grill and 75 bedrooms.

Colgate Maroon, September 22, 1970

MORE DISCUSSION ON THE PROJECT

Further discussion has taken place in regards to a proposed new facility at Seven Oaks. $1.2–1.7 million is the cost of the project at present. An architect's rendering was presented to the Council.

[*As of the January 15, 1971, meeting of the Board of Trustees, the name Colgate Athletic Council was changed to the Trustees' Committee on Athletic Affairs.*]

Colgate Athletic Council Meeting, September 25, 1970

SEVEN OAKS TO HOST JUNIOR AND PRO GOLFERS

Seven Oaks will host the 1st Annual National Junior Golfers Association Championship on August 30–September 1. The event, a 54-hole medal play championship, will have a field of 170 boys and girls under 19 years of age.

On Monday, August 30, at 2:30 p.m., touring pros Dewitt Weaver and Bunky Henry will play an exhibition with Paul Bumann, (the Clown Prince of golf as well as trick shot artist) and Ron Ryan of Colgate University.

The community is invited. There is no admission fee, but donations for Community Memorial Hospital will be accepted.

Mid-York Weekly, August 26, 1971

TOURNEY SITE AT SEVEN OAKS

Seven Oaks Golf Course, Colgate University's championship layout, will see plenty of action Saturday as the site of one of four regional qualifying tournaments in the E.C.A.C. fall schedule.

The golfing Parnell family. Pictured from the left: Marilyn, Tom, Tom, Jr., Sandy, Kathy, Jon, and Charlie. The children were all excellent players. Photo courtesy of the Thomas Parnell Collection.

OUR SEVEN OAK TREES AND PLAQUE

As we walk toward the 10th tee from the roadway, we see the beautiful arrangement of seven oak trees signifying the original home community of the Colgate family in Kent, England. In front of this grouping of trees is a plaque which gives a brief history of our golf course. The trees and plaque were gifts from the Class of '23 at their 50th Reunion. As the trees have matured, it has become a focal point for both golfers and travelers on Payne Street.

50th Reunion of the Colgate Class of '23, 1973

Fifty collegiate teams from New York and Pennsylvania will compete in a one day tournament, hoping to qualify for the fall championship scheduled for October 16 at nearby Cooperstown Country Club.

Seven Oaks Professional and Colgate golf coach Tom Parnell is tournament chairman for the event. Each team will play five men in the tourney with the winners determined by total team score for 18 holes.

Utica Observer-Dispatch, October 10, 1971

DETAILS OF THE PROPOSED MOTEL AT SEVEN OAKS

As stated by University officials recently, the plans for the new restaurant and motel at the Seven Oaks Golf Course are as follows:

The proposed plans would include 3 two-story octagonal structures connected by passageways. Each octagon would be approximately 60 feet across. One part of the complex would be made up of a dining area on the upper floor and men's and women's locker rooms for golfers on the first floor. The other two units would be used for over night accommodations; 16 of these in each octagon. The present Clubhouse would be demolished for the new dining area and motel rooms and a new Pro Shop would be built on the south side of Payne Street, at the eastern edge of the first tee area.

Mid-York Weekly, September 20, 1973

Update on an Inn at the Golf Course

Colgate University does not plan to reopen the Colgate Inn in its present condition and it has not yet decided to encourage a new inn to be built on the Seven Oaks Golf Course site, according to Raymond Krehel. The University became the owner of the inn as a result of a court-directed auction at which Colgate was the only bidder.

Commenting on the unfortunate impression which has been created within the community that the University decided to close the Colgate Inn and to build a new inn at Seven Oaks, Krehel said, "It is important that all concerned understand what the situation actually is, including the background and the history of the problem which must be solved."

He added, "No matter if one is for or against a new facility at Seven Oaks or for or against a renovated Colgate Inn, almost everyone agrees that our village has long needed good facilities for overnight accommodations, meals, and drinks for both guests of the community and for the students."

"For the past ten years there has not been an acceptable hotel in the village. Great pressure has been brought on Colgate to do something about the problem. Four or five years ago a group of private investors became interested in financing a hotel facility in Hamilton. Attracted by the natural beauty of Seven Oaks, they decided on that location in their planning. This group would have to not only be willing to put up the initial capital to build the facility, but also to shoulder any operating deficit which might develop. Colgate would merely lease the site to them."

Krehel added, however, that during the past year the project at the Seven

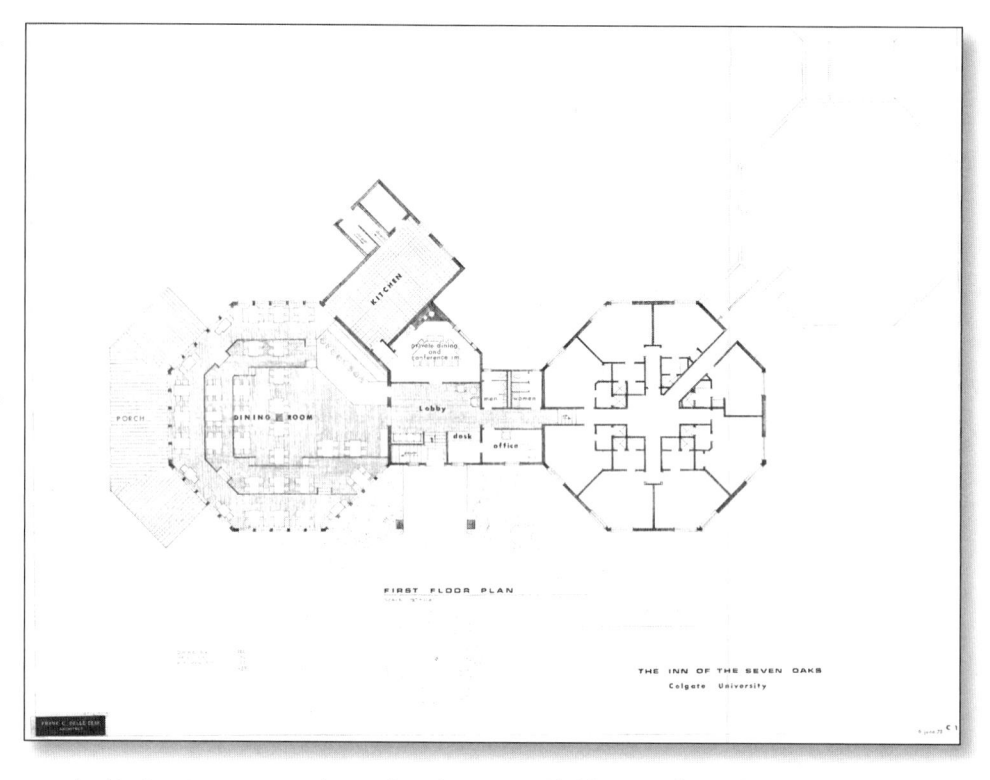

At this time it was proposed to replace the current Clubhouse and Pro Shop with the building complex pictured above. The octagon design was presented to the University for consideration. Photo courtesy of Colgate University Buildings and Grounds Collection.

Oaks site "shifted from a totally private one to a University undertaking, with the understanding that the financing would come from borrowed capital and from gifts. Some prospective donors have been found for the Seven Oaks project."

When it became evident that the University was to eventually acquire the Colgate Inn, the Board of Trustees asked the administration to consider both sites in terms of how best to meet the needs of the community. Independent studies were made and they concluded that to reopen the dining and tavern parts of the Colgate Inn would cost at least $150,000 and more than $500,000 more if good overnight accommodations were to be included.

"The interest from the community to preserve the Colgate Inn is considerable and a number of pledges have been offered by people in the village. However, sufficient funds are not yet in sight for either project. When the new joint committee of University and village representatives has explored all of the possibilities, its findings will be presented to all segments of the community."

[*New sets of plans were presented in July, September, and October of 1975. The Clubhouse would remain and a two-story addition would be constructed on the east side or north side of the building as shown in the various sets of plans. The Pro Shop would be demolished in all sets of plans and in one plan a cart shed was to be built in the northeast corner of the parking lot area. Shortly after October of 1975, the plan for this facility at Seven Oaks was abandoned. From 1994–1997 additional architectural plans were drawn for possible Clubhouse renovations and for a new Pro Shop building.*]

Madison County Times, November 8, 1973

Gilles Gagnon was appointed Head Golf Professional at Seven Oaks in 1975 following the departure of Thomas Parnell. Gagnon was an extremely good golfer, as well as hockey player. Photo courtesy of the Colgate University Sports Information Office.

GAGNON GETS COLGATE GOLF, HOCKEY POSTS

Gilles E. Gagnon, former hockey career scoring record holder at Michigan State University and a top amateur golfer, has been appointed to the dual position of head professional at Colgate University's Seven Oaks Golf Course and assistant varsity hockey coach. Gagnon, 27, will begin his duties immediately, according to Robert C. Deming, Director of Athletics.

Gagnon has been regarded as one of the top amateur players in the state of Michigan and scored 153 points while a member of the Michigan State University men's hockey team.

Utica Observer-Dispatch, April 6, 1975

NEW SEVEN OAKS FLAGPOLE

A new flagpole and American flag have been donated by the Ladies' Nine-Hole Group. The pole has been set and the flag proudly flies in the area between the Pro Shop and the Clubhouse. It is dedicated in memory of Corrine Beecher, a long-time member of the golfing group.

Mid-York Weekly, August 28, 1975

State Champions to Appear in Barnes Tourney

A strong field, including three former New York State Amateur champions, will tee off Saturday and Sunday in the third annual Eppy Barnes Best Ball Invitational Golf Tournament at Colgate University's Seven Oaks Golf Course.

Dr. Allen Foster of Syracuse, the 1975 State Amateur Champion, along with Don Allen of Rochester, a six-time state titlist and Syracuse's Nick Raasch, who won the state crown in 1967, are entered in the 74-team medal play event.

Allen will again team with Steve Carman of Seven Oaks. That duo won the event last year, posting a 36-hole total of 140 over the 6,915 yard layout.

Utica Observer-Dispatch, September 11, 1975

Colgate to Host N.C.A.A. Golf Championships

In anticipation of the national spotlight focusing on Colgate University, host of the N.C.A.A. Championships in June, steps are underway to improve the campus facilities, golf course and the college's all-round image. The 80th annual tournament will be conducted June 8–11.

[*The tournament bid had been made in June of 1975 by Dave Leonard, the Colgate Sports Information Director.*]

Bob Deming, Associate Athletic Director at Colgate, reported, "This is the first time the event is being held in a rural area. Usually the tourney is set in a western metropolis area where the weather is more dependable and better facilities available."

Housing for most of the players, coaches and families will be on the Colgate campus. The media and general public will have a choice of area hotels and motels.

About 75 colleges will be represented either in a five-man team or by sending individuals. Heading the list of college teams is Brigham Young, Wake Forest, Arizona State, University of Georgia, Ohio State, San Diego State, University of Southern California and Oklahoma State, last year's team winner at Albuquerque, New Mexico.

Scott Simpson of the University of Southern California will be on hand to defend the individual championship he won last year. Other past winners who have gone on to

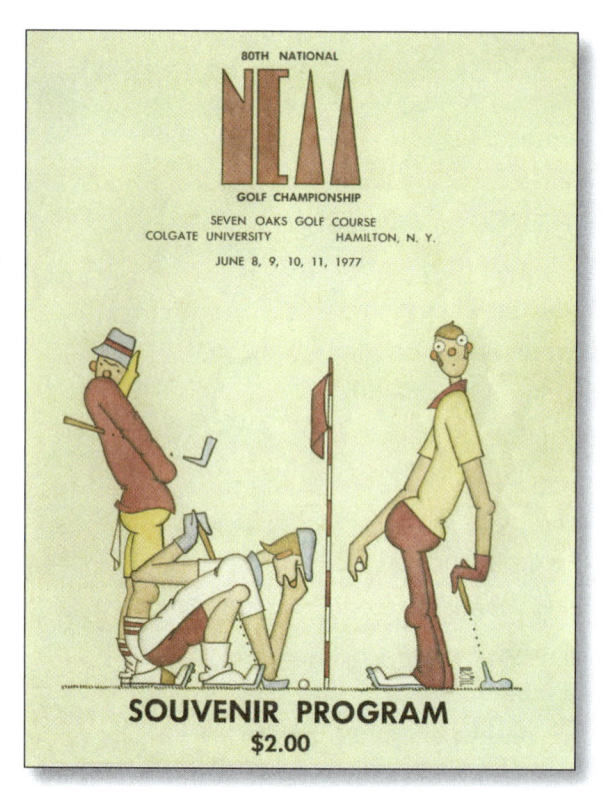

The cover for the N.C.A.A. Golf Championship booklet. The event was held at Seven Oaks in 1977. Scott Simpson, of the University of Southern California, defended his individual title and the University of Houston won the team title. The golfing cartoon on the cover was designed by Russell Fudge, a personal friend of Robert and Jean Deming. Booklet cover photo courtesy of the Richard Carroll Collection.

Russell Fudge created this cartoon golfer to be used at the 1977 N.C.A.A. Golf Championship Tournament. It was featured on posters for admission prices, registration area, parking fees, cart crossings, and others. The cartoon was also used on the menu at the Seven Oaks Clubhouse for many years. Cartoon photo courtesy of the Robert Deming Collection.

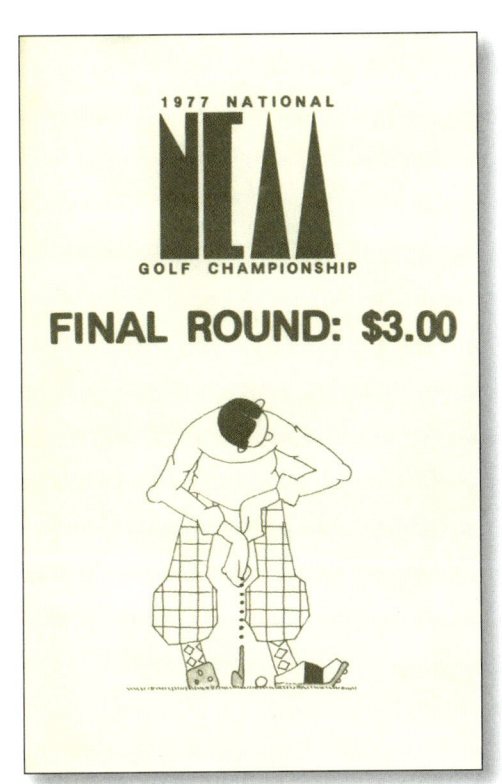

fame on the professional tour include Jack Nicklaus, Kermit Zarley, Bob Murphy, Hale Irwin, Grier Jones, John Mahaffey, Ben Crenshaw and Tom Kite.

Robert Trent Jones, who designed the challenging Seven Oaks course, will be the guest speaker at the tournament's opening banquet Tuesday night at 7 p.m. in Reid Athletic Center. Twelve hours later the first golfer will tee off in quest of national fame.

[*Prior to the tournament, Seven Oaks had only the lower putting green. N.C.A.A. Tournament officials deemed it necessary for Colgate to install the upper putting green before tournament play.*]

Utica Daily Press, June 5, 1977, and *Utica Observer-Dispatch,* April 7, 1977

SIMPSON, UNIVERSITY OF HOUSTON WIN TOURNEY

Defending champion Scott Simpson, of the University of Southern California, extended his reign over the collegiate golf world yesterday with a final round one-over-par 73 to win the 80th Annual N.C.A.A. Division I Championships.

Simpson finished with a one-over-par 289 for the four rounds. Arizona State's Lee Mikles finished second at 290 and John Stark of the University of Houston finished third with a 291.

Team honors went to the University of Houston, with Oklahoma State finishing second, Arizona State and the University of Georgia tied for third and the University of Southern California in fifth place.

[*Following the tournament, a very nice letter of thanks was sent to Colgate by Herb Wimberly, Chairman of the N.C.A.A Golf Committee. It appeared in the June 23, 1977, edition of the* Mid-York Weekly.]

Utica Observer-Dispatch, June 12, 1977

THE "PARBUSTERS" ARE FORMED

In 1978 a support group for the Colgate golf team was formed. Brad Houston had recently become the coach of the team and wanted to have a way to fund the annual spring golf trip, as well as to have a vehicle to help with projects on the Seven Oaks Golf Course. With that in mind, the Parbusters were formed.

The group's main fundraiser has been the Alumni Golf Tournament which began in 1979 and is held annually.

The tournament has evolved into an event that draws alumni from all parts of the United States for tournament competition and social events. After tournament expenses such as green fees, carts, meals, and prizes are paid, the remaining funds go to the Parbusters account.

Over the years the group has accomplished not only the funding of the spring golf trip but also the following projects for the golf course:

1. The covered bridge on #10.
2. The tall stone markers at the tee areas on all 18 holes and the forward tee on #12. The markers are labeled as having come from the Alumni Golf Tournament.
3. A water fountain at the 17th tee.
4. The scoreboard on the lawn in front of the Clubhouse.
5. The forward tee on #1.

The alumni who have played on the Colgate golf team and those who have contributed to the Parbusters fund can point with pride to the accomplishments of the group.

Information on the Parbusters from Brad Houston, Retired Colgate Golf Coach

Marian (Burke) Blain was appointed to the position of Head Golf Professional at Seven Oaks in 1982. Her tenure at the course has been marked by both courtesy and competence. This recent photo of Marian shows the extensive line of merchandise offered at the Pro Shop. Photo courtesy of the Jim Ford Collection.

APPOINTMENT OF MARIAN BURKE

Colgate University has announced the appointment of Marian Burke as Head Golf Professional at Colgate's Seven Oaks Golf Course. Burke is a native of Hamilton and graduated from Hamilton C.S. in 1973.

Marian played collegiate golf for the University of South Florida and graduated from that institution in 1979. She played mini-tour events in Florida and Ohio and also played in four L.P.G.A. events as an amateur. Marian returned to Hamilton in 1979 and has served as Assistant Head Professional for the past three years.

She will assume her duties on April 1st of this year. All members of the club are encouraged to give a warm welcome to Marian as Seven Oaks Club Professional.

Colgate Athletic Department Memo, February 1, 1982

Sand for the Bunkers

In the late 1980s a decision was made to replace the brown sand, that had been used in the bunkers since the new Seven Oaks course was opened, with the white sand that we currently see in the bunkers. It was a two-year project but certainly gives a more esthetically pleasing look that is fitting for a course of the caliber of Seven Oaks.

The course maintenance crew adds a fresh layer of sand at intervals in order to insure a proper hitting surface from our bunkers.

[*Proposals such as this have often come from the U.S. Golf Association's Turf Management Group, which has visited Seven Oaks on several occasions.*]

Information from Brad Houston and notes of the author

Remember Joe Shaheen??

In an article from the *Mid-York Weekly* on November 19, 1987, it stated that: "Joe Shaheen, of Sherburne, played 206 rounds of golf in 1986—just for fun! And as of November 14 of this year, Shaheen had played 210 rounds since April 19. Better still, on October 23, the 70-year-old golfer had played 157 rounds in 157 consecutive days since May 20. A 14 handicap player, Joe also had a hole-in-one in 1968."

In 1969, Mr. Shaheen said that "he had lost his golf game completely" and wanted to retire from the sport. However, Tom Parnell, golf pro at Seven Oaks at the time, took over and helped him get his game back and return to the sport that he loved.

Mid-York Weekly, November 19, 1987

The Seven Oaks Clubhouse and Pro Shop, Spring of 1985. The Pro Shop structure had been built for the 1977 N.C.A.A. Tournament. Photo courtesy of Special Collections and University Archives, Colgate University Libraries.

He Beat His Own Record

Joe Shaheen golfed 192 consecutive days during 1989. He stated that he wanted to thank Marian Burke, the club pro, for keeping him informed of weather conditions and tournament conflicts. He said with a smile that her weather predicting averaged about 10% correct. When asked how much his game had improved, he took the 5th.

Mid-York Weekly, November 30, 1989

Sayings of Joe Shaheen

Joe Shaheen is remembered as one of the most colorful members of Seven Oaks. He and his wife owned Shaheen's Liquor Store in Sherburne. Over the years he coined a number of phrases that can still be heard repeated at the course. Dick Carroll, a current member of the club, created a list of 45 of Joe's famous statements. The following is a sampling of that list of 45.

- *"Right in the middle on the right side."*
- (While playing early in the morning) *"Take your time—I've got until 10 o'clock tonight."*
- *"That's your best shot today—on this hole."*
- *"Nice swing—You must not have worked as a kid."*
- *"Prime location—Just like Shaheen's Liquors."*
- *"It'll be a good lie if I get there first."*
- *"Just play your own game; don't try to keep up with me!"*
- *"Man is like steel; once he loses his temper, he loses his worth."*
- *"Ah come on now! That putt should have gone in! I'm counting it!"*
- *"Just tell me what I owe."*

Leagues and Yearly Events Held at Seven Oaks

The Handicap Tournament, Jerome Handicap Cup. Began in 1919.

The Interfraternity Tournament, George W. Cobb Memorial Cup. Began in 1919.

Alumni Tournament. Began c.1930. The modern Alumni Tournament began in 1979 through the efforts of the Parbusters.

Madison County Roundup. Began in 1935. Discontinued during WWII and reactivated in 1957.

Squires vs. Captains Tournament. Began in 1936.

Men's Club Championship, Davison Trophy. Began in 1928. Not held during the early years of the Great Depression and during WWII.

Women's Club Championship, Pioneer Trophy. Began in 1928. Not held during the early years of the Great Depression and during WWII.

Women's Handicap Tournament, Wheeler Cup. Began c.1936.

Men's Handicap Tournament, Reid Cup. Began in 1936.

Scotch Foursome Tournaments. Began c.1940.

Men's Twilight League. Began in June of 1953. Ended in the late 1980s.

Mixed Couples League. Ended in the early 1990s.

Joe Huther Junior Golf Tournament. Began in 1962 as the Junior Golf Tournament through the efforts of Jim Dalgety. Renamed the Joe Huther Tournament in 1972. Ended in 1993.

Hospital Jamboree Tournament. Began in 1965. Raised funds for Community Memorial Hospital. The Men's winner received the P.T. Noyes Trophy and the Women's winner the Oneida Silversmiths Trophy. Ended in 1974.

Valley Friends Golf Tournament. Began in 1967. Sponsored by Colgate's Society of Valley Friends. Ended in 1970.

Vendetta Tournament. Began in 1971. Continues today.

Roberts Tournament. Began 1972. Continues today.

"Eppy" Barnes Invitational Best Ball Tournament. Began in 1973. Ended in 2000.

Harry Curtis Memorial Tournament. Held for a brief number of years following the death of Harry Curtis.

Herman Reynolds Senior Women's Tournament. Began in 1975. Ended in 1988.

Fred Dunlap Tournament. Began in 1997. Continues today.

Terry Slater Memorial Tournament. Began in 1992. Continues today.

Member-Member Tournament. Continues today but has not been held each year.

Men's Member-Guest Tournament. Began in 1959. Continues today.

Ladies Nine-Hole League. The league sponsored the Dalgety, Barnes, and Godfrey Tournaments. The Dalgety Tournament began in 1981, the Barnes Tournament in 1980, and the Godfrey Tournament in 1992. Ended in 2012.

Ladies Eighteen-Hole League. Continues today.

Ladies Invitational Tournament. Began in 1991. Replaced the Ladies Member-Guest Tournament.

Marian Blain and research of the author

Seven Oaks Scorecard c. 1990. The Blue, White, and Red Courses of the day have been replaced by the present-day Black, Maroon, White, and Grey courses. Courtesy of the Seven Oaks Pro Shop.

81

EIGHT: THE 1990S TO THE PRESENT

THE HOGAN TOUR EVENT

Seven Oaks was selected as one of the sites for the Ben Hogan Tour in 1990. The official name of the event was the Ben Hogan Central New York Classic. It was certainly an honor for Seven Oaks and an opportunity to display our beautiful and challenging course.

In all, 132 golfers were entered in the field of competitors. They were selected based on 15 criteria such as being the winner of a previous Hogan Tour event, selection by the P.G.A. of America, being a top finisher in a Hogan Tour regional qualifying event, or being selected by the host P.G.A section, just to name a few.

The golfers soon realized that the layout of the Robert Trent Jones designed course was difficult to say the least. By the end of three rounds only 27 golfers had shot under par. Individual rounds could be a different story, however, as Jim McGovern tied a Seven Oaks course record with a round of 66. The unusual thing about his record round is that he started off with a bogey on #1.

The eventual winner of the tournament was Tom Garner of Winter Park, Florida. He posted a score of 207 beating out Andrew Morse, Ed Humenik, and Brian Watts, who all finished with 208. Jim McGovern and Tom Lehman followed with scores of 209.

[*The name of the tour was later changed to the Nike Tour and then to the current name, the Nationwide Tour.*]

Tournament results from Brad Houston, Retired Colgate Golf Coach

CONSTRUCTION OF THE FORWARD TEES

In 1995 the idea of forward tees for some holes on the course was pushed ahead. The thought behind these extra teeing areas was to help senior players, the ladies of our club, and our young players. This would insure them the opportunity to post good scores during their round of golf on an equal footing with the long hitters who had no trouble with the distances of our many challenging holes. The concept had been put into place at many golfing venues across the United States.

Plans were discussed and bids made in July of 1996, with ideas finalized in September of that year. The contract was given to A. John Harvey of The Golf Group, Inc., from Bernardston, Massachusetts. The plan was for construction to begin in the fall of 1996.

The proposal from The Golf Group, Inc., called for forward tees on 16 of the 18 holes of the course. Holes #2 and #14 would not have a forward tee. When plans were

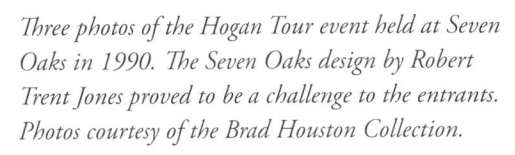

Three photos of the Hogan Tour event held at Seven Oaks in 1990. The Seven Oaks design by Robert Trent Jones proved to be a challenge to the entrants. Photos courtesy of the Brad Houston Collection.

finalized and construction began, forward tees were built on 12 of the 18 holes. Holes 2, 3, 8, 13, 14, and 17 would not have a forward tee built.

Under the direction of A. John Harvey, "Stub" Baker, a local excavating contractor, did the heavy work. The tees are constructed of topsoil with a strong mixture of sand blended in. The new tees were ready for play in 1997.

Documents from the Colgate Athletic Office and Marian (Burke) Blain

The Naming of the Forward Tees at Seven Oaks

The naming of the twelve forward tees is detailed in the following list.

1 This forward tee is given by the Parbusters. The Parbusters are the Alumni and friends of the Colgate University Golf Team.

4 Given by Jaye and George Parsons '64.

5 In memory of James J. Mahoney and Warren E. Eaton by Polly Roberts Mahoney and Jane Roberts Eaton.

6 Given by members of Seven Oaks in tribute to Marian Burke Blain for all she has done to promote the game of golf.

7 In recognition of former Colgate University Athletic Director Harold Lahar for all his efforts in making Seven Oaks a reality.

9 In honor of A. Theodore Persson '42 and Helen K. Persson H'84 in recognition of their support of Colgate and Seven Oaks.

10 Given by Marilyn and Fred Dunlap '50.

11 Given by the Women's Athletic Alliance, which supports Colgate University's women's teams.

15 Given in memory of Joe Huther '29 by Cornelia Huther and Bill Huther '56. A great friend of Colgate and Seven Oaks.

16 Given in memory of Dr. Stanley E. Baldwin '12 by Everett N. Baldwin '54 and Gary E. Baldwin '91.

18 Enjoy! Betsy and Ed Vantine '56.

[*The forward tee on #12 has a marker donated by the Alumni Golf Tournament along with the other 18 markers that grace each tee box area and give a colored picture of each hole. The forward tee on #12 marked the original tee box on #9 before the back nine was constructed and our current 9th hole was moved to its present location on the course.*]

Research of the Author

TIFFANY'S TERRACE

The terrace area behind the Clubhouse, which presents a spectacular view of the "back six" holes of the course, was dedicated on July 11, 1997, "In memory of Donald L. Tiffany '43 by Tiff's family and friends." For anyone who has enjoyed a drink and meal on the terrace, it is a special place to spend time while at the course.

Plaque at Tiffany Terrace and notes of the author

U.S.G.A., E.C.A.C., AND N.C.A.A. EVENTS HELD AT SEVEN OAKS

- **1963, 1975 N.Y.S. Junior Girls Championship.** Won by Carolyn Ploysa in 1963 and Cynthia Pietrusik in 1975.
- **1964, 1971, 1982, 1986, 1987, 1988, 1989, and 1994 E.C.A.C. Fall Golf Championship.** [*This tournament uses a number of sites for the qualifier. Colgate was chosen as one of four qualifying sites.*]
- **1967 N.Y.S. Girls Amateur Championship.** Won by Doll Story.
- **1971 N.Y.S. Junior Boys Championship.** Winner of 14 and under age group won was Joey Sindelar, 15–17 age group won by Don Kalode.
- **1971 Junior Golfers Association National Tournament**
- **1976 Boy's State Amateur Tournament.** Won by John Ryan.
- **1977 N.C.A.A National Championship Tournament.** Won by Scott Simpson of the University of Southern California.
- **1983 Women's State Amateur Tournament.** Won by Mary Anne Widman.
- **1988 North Atlantic Conference Championship**

84

- **1990 Ben Hogan Central New York Classic.** Won by Tom Garner.
- **1992 N.C.A.A. D-1 Men's Golf Championship, East Regional.** Won by Jimmy Johnston of Georgia Tech.
- **1993, 2001 Men's State Amateur Tournament.** Won by Jeffrey Peck in 1993 and Kevin Haefner in 2001.
- **Senior Open Qualifier** has been held three times at Seven Oaks.
- **Section Three High School Tournament Qualifier.** Held yearly at Seven Oaks. Lowest eight scorers then participate in the State Championships at the Robert Trent Jones Course at Cornell.
- **2010 Patriot League Championship.** Held on a rotating basis at Patriot League courses. Seven Oaks hosts the tournament every five years.

Marian Blain and research of the author

THE PERKIN-SUMPTION PRACTICE AREA

In 2005 a new driving range facility was built on the hill northeast of the course. It overlooks the Village of Hamilton and the beautiful Chenango Valley. The original driving range, located across the street from the Pro Shop and the Clubhouse, was deemed to be too small for the current game. It also offered no short game area for members, guests, and the Colgate Golf Team to use. The new site would have adequate space for all of these activities, plus a small building to house a golf ball dispensing machine, bathroom, and water cooler.

The project was pushed forward through the efforts of Athletic Director Mark Murphy and Course Superintendent Peter Sermini. The University contacted the Jordan Golf Design Company to draw up a plan for the new range. Local excavating contractor, "Stub" Baker, was hired to do the initial road construction and the bulldozing work

The design plan for the Perkin-Sumption practice facility. You can see that the original plan featured a lower tee area also. The facility offers fantastic views of the Colgate campus and the Chenango Valley. Photo courtesy of the Marian Blain Collection.

for the practice area. Seven Oaks Golf Course personnel did the finished work.

The new range was opened for use in 2006 and has provided not only a practice area to improve your game, but a spectacular view as well.

Notes of the author

Is It Green or Greens??

The words "Green" and "Greens" have popped up many times in the research for this account of the history of Seven Oaks Golf Course. In conversations with golf officials and sources from internet articles, the following is some information which can put the controversy to rest.

According to a statement from the *U.S.G.A. Journal*, the biggest mistake in golf terminology is the confusion of "Green" and "Greens."

We go back to the British Isles to find the origin of the word "Green." In Britain, a "Green" referred to the Village Green. Often this area was hundreds of acres in size. It was divided into grazing land, community crop land, and a recreational area. Over time this recreational area became a golf course at some of the Village Green locations.

The idea of a Village Green was brought to the United States by our early settlers. It was an area for cattle and sheep to graze, and in our early history militia drills were conducted on the Green. Many communities continue to have a Green. Hamilton has a wonderful example of a Village Green, as do many other neighboring communities such as Clinton, Peterboro, and Oriskany Falls.

As the term pertains to golf courses, we focus on the recreational aspects of the word. We have a manager of the lands upon which the golf course was constructed. That person is known as the "Greenkeeper" or the keeper of the "Green." We have a "Green Committee" which oversees and gives ideas concerning the upkeep of the "Green." When we arrive at the course, we pay a "Green Fee" meaning a fee for the privilege of playing a round of golf on the entire "Green." And of course we use the term, "Through the Green."

In any case the word is singular because the word "Green" is singular. It is a common error and one that we all have made.

United States Golf Association Journal and notes of the author

Colgate University Seven Oaks Club Championship Winners

Year	Men	Women
1928	William Reid	Prudence Hawkins
1929	William Reid	Kathryn Williams
1930–32	*No Tournament, early years of the Great Depression*	
1933	William Reid	*No Women's Tournament*
1934	Warren Alton	*No Women's Tournament*
1935	Rev. C.T. Holcombe	Prudence Hawkins
1936	John D. MacQueen	Prudence Hawkins
1937	J. Leslie Hart	Prudence Hawkins
1938	J. Leslie Hart	Irene Ravette
1939	J. Leslie Hart	Irene Ravette
1940	William L. Burke	Jean C. Davis
1941	Frances A. Gahan	*No Women's Tournament*
1942–50	*No Tournament during WWII and shortly after*	
1951	Frank J. O'Hora	Thelma Barnes

Year	Men	Women
1952	William L. Burke	Daisy Roberts
1953	William L. Burke	Daisy Roberts
1954	William L. Burke	Lenore Reynolds
1955	Robert Hahnle	Thelma Barnes
1956	William L. Burke	Mary Ann Fitzpatrick
1957	Paul Lambert	Mary Ann Fitzpatrick
1958	William L. Burke	Helen Spooner
1959	Robert O'Hora	Pat Shirley
1960	Frank J. O'Hora	Mary Ann Fitzpatrick
1961	Robert O'Hora	Pat Shirley
1962	Hal Lahar	Pat Shirley
1963	Hal Lahar	Pat Shirley
1964	William L. Burke	Jane Eaton
1965	Hal Lahar	Catherine Stradling
1966	Ron Ryan	Catherine Stradling
1967	Ron Ryan	Jane Eaton
1968	Hal Lahar	Jane Eaton
1969	Hal Lahar	Jane Eaton
1970	Ron Ryan	Sally Sanders
1971	Frank Potter	Marian Burke (Blain)
1972	Hal Lahar	Polly Cooley (Mahoney)
1973	Frank Southfield	Sandy Parnell
1974	George Homokay	Martha Wade
1975	Frank Potter	Marian Burke (Blain)
1976	Frank Potter	Marian Burke (Blain)
1977	Bill Gerber	Jane Eaton
1978	Marty Erb	Jane Eaton
1979	Don Davidson	Jane Eaton
1980	Gary Rider	Patti Butcher
1981	Marty Erb	Jane Eaton
1982	Mark Kunkel	Jane Eaton
1983	Mark DeMellier	Jane Eaton
1984	Ed Vantine	Jana DeVencenzo
1985	Dick Carroll	Jana DeVencenzo
1986	Brad Houston	Jana DeVencenzo
1987	Steve Upton	Jana DeVencenzo
1988	Bob Tyburski	Jana DeVencenzo
1989	Drew Fiumano	Jane Eaton
1990	Dick Carroll	Jane Eaton
1991	Steve Espe	Marilyn Dunlap
1992	Drew Fiumano	Jane Eaton
1993	Bob Modliszewski	Marilyn Dunlap
1994	Bob Modliszewski	Polly Mahoney
1995	Chris Lura	Marilyn Dunlap
1996	John P. Blain	Marilyn Dunlap
1997	Al Cafruny	Marilyn Dunlap
1998	Ted Wampfler	Marilyn Dunlap
1999	Ron Czyzycki	Marilyn Dunlap
2000	John P. Blain	Jane Eaton
2001	Ron Czyzycki	Marilyn Dunlap
2002	Steve Espe	Marilyn Dunlap
2003	Ron Czyzycki	Jane Eaton
2004	Keith Tyburski	Debby Hepburn
2005	Steve Espe	Marilyn Dunlap
2006	Steve Espe	Debby Hepburn
2007	John Hawley	Debby Hepburn
2008	John P. Blain	Carly McNaughton
2009	Kevin Lojewski	Carly McNaughton
2010	John Hawley	Debby Hepburn
2011	Joseph S. Hope	Debby Hepburn
2012	Joseph S. Hope	Eileen Albanese

Research by Marian Blain and the author

Our Current Course Transformation

If we look closely at the projects undertaken by Robert Trent Jones over his long career, it soon becomes evident that he not only designed courses but was also hired to make redesigns. Every course needs changes as the years go by. These might be in the form of drainage, repair of bunkers, the removal or addition of trees, and the lengthening of tees.

In recent years Colgate University has begun the process of assessing the future needs of Seven Oaks. This thought process led to the hiring of Forse Design, Inc., in 2010 to make recommendations for projects to address the needs of our course and to design a plan for those changes. Jim Nagle has been assigned by the company as the chief design specialist.

Their assessment has so far looked like the above list of changes that courses may need. Drainage heads the list of necessary projects, followed by tree removal, bunker repair, restoring the size and shape of the greens to their original dimensions, repairs to the putting green, and the leveling of tee boxes.

In the upcoming years we will follow with great interest how these ideas from Forse Design will be implemented at Seven Oaks.

Information from Marian Blain and design ideas from Forse Design, Inc.

Seven Oaks Club Professionals, Old and New Course

- James Dalgety — 1928–1962
- Thomas Parnell — 1963–1974
- Gilles Gagnon — 1975–1980
- Francis "Buddy" Powers — 1981
- Marian (Burke) Blain — 1982–Present

[*2013 marks Marian's 31st year of service to Seven Oaks*]

Seven Oaks Course Superintendents, New Course Only

- Harold Dahn, 1957–1974 [*Llewellyn Lamb, Jr., was assigned to work with Dahn in 1965. Harold Dahn had been the superintendent of the "hill" course also.*]
- Harry Curtis, 1973–1975 [*Harry served with Harold Dahn in 1973 and early 1974*]
- Dave Geiger, 1976–1978
- 1979–1982, Personnel from University Buildings and Grounds were assigned to oversee the course
- Roger Galler, 1983–1986
- Eric Ogren, 1987–part of 1995
- Ranjit Sangramsingh, part of 1995–1996
- Greg Wall, 1997–2001 [*Remainders of 2001 and 2005 seasons*]
- Peter Sermini, 2002–2005
- Jon McConville, 2006–Present

Marian Blain and research of the author

A Note on Jon McConville

Seven Oaks has been very fortunate to have qualified course superintendents over the years. Through their vision, many positive changes have occurred which have made our course a wonderful golfing experience.

With the hiring of Jon McConville in 1996, Seven Oaks has moved into a new and exciting phase of development. Jon has become known throughout Central New York for his attention to the greens. Their condition and speed is truly remarkable. Coupled with a new range of pin placements and height of the rough, a golfer has to be totally concentrated in order to score well. It is a challenge that enthusiasts of the game truly look forward to.

The grounds crew that Jon has assembled shows a high degree of professionalism and each member takes a great deal of pride in his work. These traits have certainly shown themselves to be true in the current condition of Seven Oaks.

Observations of the author

Jon McConville is the current (2013) Head Groundskeeper at Seven Oaks. His skills are apparent in the condition of the course and especially in his attention to the greens. He and his crew do a marvelous job each summer. Photo courtesy of the Jim Ford Collection.

Tee It Forward

The P.G.A. of America and the United States Golf Association have developed a program known as "Tee It Forward." The purpose of the program is to enable players to determine the correct course yardage to play based on the average distance of their drive. For example, if you hit a drive 275 yards consistently, the recommended 18-hole yardage for you is between 6,700 and 6,900 yards. Our course is 6,915 yards from the championship tees. These golfers would be using the black tees. But unless you can strike your drive 275 yards consistently, you should probably consider the maroon tees and not the black.

In another example, if you hit your drive 200 yards, the ideal length of the course for you is 5,200 to 5,400 yards. On our course you would have a much better experience using the white markers on the tee, and even those might be a little too much length for your game.

What is the purpose you might ask? Many of us think that we are using the right tees for our game, when in actuality we are making the game too hard. We cannot comfortably reach the green in the desired number of strokes. If we did play the correct tees, we could reach the green and have more fun at the same time. For our senior golfers, many of our ladies, and for the junior golfers at our course, this is a great idea. Make the game fun and enjoy your social time with others without trying to reach distances beyond your current ability.

Information from "Tee It Forward" bulletin, courtesy of Marian Blain

A Short Biography of Marian (Burke) Blain

- Born in Syracuse and raised in Hamilton, New York
- Daughter of William Burke, Jr., and granddaughter of William Burke, Sr. William Sr. was instrumental in the development of the original Seven Oaks course on the hill. William Jr. was a proponent of a full championship course, which resulted in our current course.
- Graduated from Hamilton Central School in 1973.
- First female to participate on a boy's varsity team at Hamilton C.S.
- Was a four-year member of the boy's varsity golf team at Hamilton C.S.
- Played collegiate golf at the University of South Florida.
- Graduated from the University of South Florida in 1979.
- Played mini-tour events in Florida and Ohio and played in four L.P.G.A. events as an amateur.
- Returned to Hamilton in 1979 and served as Assistant at Seven Oaks from 1979–1981.
- Was appointed Head Golf Professional at Colgate University's Seven Oaks Golf Course, April 1, 1982. Has now served in that capacity for 31 years.
- Only James Dalgety served a longer tenure as golf professional at Colgate.
- First female to become a P.G.A. member in the Central New York P.G.A. Section.
- Has headed the village recreation golf program for 31 years.
- 1992 Received the Central New York P.G.A. Professional of the Year Award for contributions to the game.
- 1992 Received a Colgate Maroon Council Citation for loyalty and service to Colgate.
- 1993 Named the Central New York P.G.A. Merchandiser of the Year for demonstrating skills in merchandising in the promotion of golf.
- 1998 Received the Central New York P.G.A. Horton Smith Award, which recognized Marian as a model educator of P.G.A. Professionals.
- 2004 Named the Central New York P.G.A. Women's Player of the Year in recognition of her expertise as a golfer and her performance at Seven Oaks.
- 2005–2007 Colgate University Head Men's Golf Coach.
- 2011 Named as the Central New York P.G.A. Merchandiser of the Year.
- 2012 Induction into the Central New York P.G.A. Hall of Fame.
- Resides in Hamilton with her husband, John, and daughter Bridget.

Information from Marian Blain and Colgate University

Marian Blain has been the head pro at Seven Oaks for the past 31 years. In that time she has made a reputation for customer service, courtesy, and extreme knowledge of the game. We wish her more successful years at Seven Oaks. Photo courtesy of the Jim Ford Collection.

The Clubhouse at Seven Oaks is managed by Doug Speer and his capable staff. The facility offers an extensive menu that is bound to suit every taste. Doug is also a very fine golfer in his own right. Photo courtesy of the Jim Ford Collection.

AREA COURSES DESIGNED BY ROBERT TRENT JONES

In addition to Seven Oaks there are six other golf courses designed by Robert Trent Jones in our immediate driving distance. We could certainly have our own Robert Trent Jones Golf Trail right here in Central New York.

- Durand-Eastman Park Golf Course—Rochester
- Green Lakes State Park Golf Course—Fayetteville
- Cornell University Golf Course—Ithaca
- Midvale Golf and Country Club—Penfield
- Bristol Harbor Village Golf Club—Canandaigua
- Radisson Greens Golf Course—Baldwinsville

Other courses such as Oak Hill Country Club and Locust Hill Country Club in Rochester and Valley View Golf Course in Utica are examples of Jones' remodeling efforts. Information from the Robert Trent Jones Society

THE CLUBHOUSE AT SEVEN OAKS

The historic Dr. Wheeler home serves as the Clubhouse at Seven Oaks Golf Course. Owned by Colgate University, it is currently leased to Doug Speer, who operates a family-owned restaurant on the premises.

Doug is a graduate of Hamilton Central School and a 1994 graduate of the University of South Florida. He played two years on the mini-tour before moving to the Washington, D.C., area. It was there that he entered the restaurant trade.

The Clubhouse offers a menu to suit every taste, from a sandwich following a round of golf to a formal array of unique entrees served in the beautiful dining room. The views are spectacular from the enclosed porch or from the outdoor seating area known as Tiffany Terrace.

Doug and his able staff have created an atmosphere that is inviting to both the Hamilton and Colgate communities. If you haven't as yet had the privilege, please try this unique dining experience at Seven Oaks.

Detail of Design Plan #3—one of several plans drawn to complement the nine holes "on the hill" in the mid-1950s. Map photo courtesy of Colgate University Buildings and Grounds Collection.

Play is governed by USGA Rules of Golf

Course Rating/Slope
Black   74.6/143
Maroon   71.6/135
White   68.8/124
Grey   71.6/128

Colgate University
Seven Oaks G.C.
East Lake & Payne Streets • Hamilton, NY 13346
(315) 824-1432
www.sevenoaksgolf.com

Colgate University
Seven Oaks Golf Club

Course Designed by: Robert Trent Jones

Holes	1	2	3	4	5	6	7	8	9	Out	10	11	12	13	14	15	16	17	18	In	Tot	Hcp	Net	Adj
Black Course	433	149	378	385	516	441	528	183	452	3465	380	221	528	362	180	426	444	363	546	3450	6915			
Maroon Course	405	126	345	363	466	433	510	161	432	3241	356	192	507	337	148	393	407	329	513	3182	6423			
White Course	391	123	340	346	403	418	450	150	381	3002	337	167	431	326	130	365	375	310	466	2907	5909			
Par	4	3	4	4	5	4	5	3	4	36	4	3	5	4	3	4	4	4	5	36	72			
Handicap	3	17	15	9	13	1	7	11	5		2	8	12	16	14	10	4	18	6					
Grey Course	335	118	334	232	387	315	440	145	315	2621	290	125	421	316	124	320	315	300	420	2631	5252			
Par	4	3	4	4	5	4	5	3	4	36	4	3	5	4	3	4	4	4	5	36	72			
Handicap	1	17	7	13	5	9	3	15	11		2	18	8	10	16	12	6	4	14					

Courtesy of the Seven Oaks Pro Shop.

Grass, Trees, Sand, and Water

A number of scorecards have been featured in this history of Seven Oaks. We include our current scorecard above so that when changes to the course are made in the future, we will have an accurate indication of the yardages that we played in 2013. We would be remiss if we did not mention that the full name for the course is Colgate University Seven Oaks Golf Club. Colgate University is rightfully proud of its beautiful and challenging course and the reputation which it has achieved.